Mission: AFRICA
A Light Look at a Once-Dark Continent

Mission:
AFRICA
A Light Look at a Once-Dark Continent

Bob Prouty

Pacific Press Publishing Association
Boise, Idaho
Oshawa, Ontario
Montemorelos, N.L., Mexico

Cover illustration by Sue Rother

Copyright © 1984 by
Pacific Press Publishing Association
Printed in United States of America

Library of Congress Cataloging in Publication Data

Prouty, Robert.
   Mission—Africa.

   (Destiny II)
   1. Prouty, Robert. 2. Missionaries—Zaire—Biography. 3. Missionaries—Canada—Biography. I. Title.
BV3625.C63P7   1984   260'.092'4 [B]   84-7820
ISBN 0-8163-0561-7

84 85 86 87 88 89 • 6 5 4 3 2 1

Dedication

In the late 1960s, at Kingsway College, a somewhat unorthodox teacher presided over the English classes. It was not uncommon for him to teach with his feet propped up on his desk, his chair tipped back, his hands clasped behind his head, and his eyes firmly fixed on the ceiling. The administrators and the inspectors were horrified, but he knew how to teach, and we who were his students loved him. He was dedicated to us. And that's why this book is dedicated to him, Morris M. Gutman.

Contents

"Whither Thou Goest" 9
The Hippo and I 13
The Humanitarian Border Guard 17
A Backyard Glance 22
Early Days of Mission Life 28
The Trees of Lukanga Mission 33
A Sermon Goes Wrong 37
The Family on Safari 41
What's in a Name? 45
Kavis and the Nande Hymnal 50
Trivia 55
A Day to Forget 59
A Day to Remember 64
A Snake at the Baptism 69
The Missionary Goes to Court 74
The Walls Came Tumbling Down 79
Mrs. Nzabamwita's Special Sabbath Dinner 84
Home at Last! But Africa Has Our Hearts! 89

"Whither Thou Goest"

A shout, a sudden rush of water, and I was in the grip of an enormous hippo. It all happened so fast. There was no warning—no time to react. I felt no fear or panic, but I had certainly not expected anything like this when I first came to Africa.

How did I get into this predicament?

I had lived in Oshawa, a comfortable city on the shores of Lake Ontario most of my life. When Diane and I decided to marry, we searched for the just-right house in which to live. For the fifth time in five years of marriage we had moved from one house to another. But this was our big move. We were moving into a house of our very own. It came complete with new sod, an eight-foot tall white birch on the front lawn, and a thirty-year mortgage. To most people the house looked like every other house within a half-mile radius, but to us it was different. It was ours. We were proud of it and proud of ourselves. We moved in on December 15, 1977.

On December 31, some 600 miles away in Washington, D.C., Elder Bernard Seton sat in his office at the General Conference and wrote us a letter asking us to go to Africa.

Diane's reaction to the letter, when it arrived, was immediate and unequivocal. "I can't do it," she said. "I've been dreaming of this house since we were married. I can't give it up just like that." She snapped her fingers as she spoke and turned away.

We ignored the letter and fixed up the rec room in the basement of our first real home.

Early in January Bernard Seton retired, and Maurice Battle took his post of duty. Elder Battle was returning from mission service, and on his way to Washington, D.C., he came to Oshawa. He had never been there before; to my knowledge he has never been there since, but he held the Sabbath service that weekend, and he made an appeal for missionaries to go to Africa.

After the service we talked to Elder Battle; we ended up talking for several hours. By now, I was definitely interested in Africa. Diane still was not, so after much thought we decided against the idea. We finished up the rec room and bought a stove.

The subject didn't come up again for several months, and we settled ever more comfortably into our house. A brand-new dishwasher had just been purchased and installed in April. Late one night, the phone rang.

It was Washington, D.C., on the line. We were needed desperately in Africa. The official call had already been sent through the mail. Would we go? They gave us a day to think it over and pray about it. One day! Twenty-four hours!

I knew I wanted to go, but I knew Diane didn't. Time was short and I had already tried almost every means of persuasion I could think of. There was just one thing left. It was now or never, and I pulled out my trump card.

"Diane," I began, "remember your wedding vows?"

Diane stood by the sink in the kitchen. She stopped peeling the potato that she held in her hand and looked at me quizzically. She knew her wedding vows, of course. We had written them ourselves. After five years, she could repeat them as well as on our wedding day, and she hadn't missed a beat then.

"I'm not quite sure what you mean."

"Remember the part about 'whither thou goest'?" I asked.

Silence. She dropped the potato, went over to the stove, and adjusted the gas flame. I noticed the far-away look in her eyes. "Of course I remember it. I meant it too. 'Whither thou goest, I will go,' but nobody was talking about Africa then. We were talking about Canada."

"All right," I said, realizing as black smoke curled upward from the frying pan that it was no time to press my advantage, "you win."

Supper was a quiet one that night as we both were lost in thought. We were still thinking when the phone rang.

"Well, what about it, Bob? Do you think you can help us out?" The voice on the other end sounded friendly, smooth, assured. It was Don Roth of the General Conference calling.

"I don't know, Pastor Roth. We've had a hard time deciding."

"Call me Don," the voice on the other end of the line said. "Listen, Bob, I understand your hesitation. It's not an easy decision. You go right ahead and talk it over with your wife. Take all the time you need. I'll just hang on because I've got a committee here waiting for your answer. But don't worry about that and don't worry about the long distance; you're important to us."

Something more than the long distance call was worrying Diane. "How are we going to sell the house, Bob? And what about the children? You can't just run off halfway around the world with two toddlers."

My wife was right, as usual, and I conveyed her concern.

"No problem, Bob. You sell that house, and we'll wait for you."

Now I was suspicious. "I thought you needed us right away."

"We do, Bob, we do. But if you've got to sell that house,

we'll wait. Now what do you say to that, my friend?"

I looked at Diane and she looked at me with that hopeless shrug of resignation I knew so well. "OK, Pastor Roth, I guess you can put us down. We'll go."

Pastor Roth sounded ecstatic over the telephone. He didn't know us then, and he hasn't seen us since; but he made us feel that his happiness was ensured for life. He hung up the phone in a joyful mood and no doubt rushed off to the committee meeting.

There was less ecstasy on our end of the line. We looked at one another tentatively, wondering what forces we had set in motion. A phone call, a wedding vow, and we were on our way to Africa. It made you think.

The Hippo and I

Floating with the current, my head under the water, I didn't even see the hippo until it was all over. He had been swimming upstream, also under the water, surfacing only seconds before reaching me.

Some of the students saw what was happening and shouted, but by then it was too late. Coming down the bluff a quarter mile away, Gad Mwangacucu saw everything from a bird's-eye view and ran frantically down to the beach. He later told me that he didn't expect to find me alive when he got there.

His concern was not imaginary. A hippo is an immense creature, the third-largest land animal in existence. As much as fifteen feet long and weighing up to two and a half tons, its jaws can open well over a yard wide. I had already seen those open jaws and those long curving teeth many times in the few days we had spent at Ishango.

Ishango is a campsite on the shores of Lake Edward. It is on the border between Uganda and Zaire. If any other place more closely resembles the Garden of Eden, I don't know of it. Just beyond the tenting area tall bluffs drop a hundred feet to the Semliki River. A hundred yards away, where the river flows out from the lake on its journey to the Nile, flocks of pelicans and gulls spend their days fishing and flying in formation. On the far side of the river antelope wander lazily about. Great herds of hippos—dozens of them and perhaps hundreds—frequent the river, while stooped white egrets perch nonchalantly on their backs.

At night the hippos climb the steep bluffs and graze on the short grasses where our tents were pitched. Lions also wander about in the evening, but, like the hippos, they are wary of man. I had received firm assurances from the park guards that no one had been injured by these animals as far back as they could remember.

Each year while in Africa, I went with the graduating students and a few teachers for a week of fellowship and Bible study down at the lake. That year Stefan and Chuck, Lukanga's two student missionaries, had also come along to help. Chuck drove the truck; Stefan helped with the daily program. I had taken our two oldest children, Heather and Danny, along on this camping trip as well. Two days into the trip they were just as excited as they had been when we started out. They had been many places with me before, but never one like Ishango.

"Let's go swimming, Daddy. Isn't it time yet?" Heather queried.

"No, it isn't time yet," I answered, knowing how anxiously she waited to get into the water again. But our midday rest period wasn't over. Our meetings were confined to a few hours in the morning and a few hours in the evening because of the heat. Except for lunch and a rest period, the remaining hours were for swimming.

"Time yet, Daddy?" It was Heather again.

"Not yet, kids." I kept my eyes on my Italian book. I had brought it along to occupy whatever spare time I might have. I was studying it—admittedly not the most practical book for Africa—in the fond hope of surprising my Italian-speaking friends at the Catholic mission down the road from our school. I glanced at the list of verbs again. *E sopravissuto*—He has survived. They were the last words I studied before heading off to the beach with the children, and the words soon turned out to be prophetic.

The beach, about a hundred yards long, was divided roughly into three parts. One part was used by the boats. Some were equipped with motors and some were propelled through the water by long poles, but all were made of the same rough planks.

Another part of the beach was the domain of the fishermen. They would swing their nylon lines round and round over their heads, then let them go, singing far out into the river. As often as one time in three, they brought a fish to shore.

The last stretch of beach, a twenty-yard strip of weeds and sand, was reserved for bathing and swimming. A few of the students and a couple of children were in the water, laughing and splashing, when we arrived. A pelican skimmed past, wingtips lightly brushing the water. He seemed to cast an annoyed glance in our direction as he flew. Downstream, the hippos floated lazily.

As I waded a few yards out into the current, Heather and Danny raced to the end of the beach. We had done this before, and they knew the routine. I swam down to where they were waiting. Taking one by each arm, I pulled them back upstream through the shallows. They laughed and turned and ran back down the beach to wait for me again. I jumped in and let the current carry me toward them.

But that time I never reached them. A scant five yards from shore, surrounded by noisy swimmers and splashers, I ran into the hippo. Or perhaps it ran into me. Whichever it was, we came together with a jolt.

Just what the hippo was doing there at that time of day would be hard to say. Some have suggested that it was protecting its young. This may be true, although we saw no young. Others simply feel that it was a troublemaker. This also may be true, but I tend to suspect that it was just a case of the two of us being in the wrong place at the wrong time. The hippo was probably just as surprised to find me as I was to find it.

I didn't know what I had met up with at first. I thought it was one of the students and turned in the water to see what was happening. It was the best thing I could have done. We had come together head to head, but as I twisted around only my backside was exposed to those jaws. The next thing I knew, I was being lifted up and tossed about. Then, just as quickly as it had begun, it was all over. I made it to the shore and collapsed.

Instantly, Chuck, Gad, Stefan, and others were at my side, doing what they could to treat the wound. Within fifteen minutes, the bleeding had been stopped and preparations were being made to carry me up the bluff to the tenting area, where the truck was parked. Just as we were about to move off, a shout went up. I looked up and saw the hippo floating a few feet from shore, looking at me quizzically—probably wondering what all the fuss was about.

The Humanitarian Border Guard

"It is impossible, I tell you, totally impossible! As long as I am on duty, no one is going anywhere!"

"Come on, man, be reasonable. He needs to get to a hospital. Let them through, if only for humanitarian purposes."

From where I was lying on the open bed of the school truck, I could hear the voices as the argument went back and forth. We were at the Uganda-Zaïre border, an hour's drive from Ishango. I had hoped the small dispensary at the border village would have the facilities for sewing up my wounds, but it didn't. There was nothing else nearby in Zaïre, and the nurse had suggested a hospital just inside Uganda. This is what had started the argument.

I listened with only mild interest to the disembodied voices floating through the air. One evidently belonged to an official arguing the case for our side with his superior. He had a great fondness for the word *humanitarian* and repeated it time after time, as if it were some sort of talisman. His superior had an equal fondness for the word *impossible*. He would say it slowly, almost lovingly, accentuating each syllable in an exaggerated fashion, then repeating the entire word three times rapidly in staccato bursts of sound. The villagers found this highly amusing, and I could hear great laughter going up whenever he spoke. I soon realized that my presence was a matter of only minor importance in the whole affair. The discussion was for the benefit of the bystanders. I was beginning to wonder how much longer this could go on when things took a sudden turn for the better.

"Hello, what's happened to you?" The cheerful English voice jumping out at me from the sea of French was as reassuring as it was unexpected. I still could see no one, but obviously someone could see me. The question was repeated. "I say, what appears to be the problem?"

"Bottom," I said lamely. I hadn't been expecting a chance to talk and could think of nothing more appropriate to say.

"Well, that's a bit of a nuisance, I should think. Let me fetch my wife, and she'll have a go at you with some Dettol, if you like." I caught a glimpse of a big form jumping down from the truck. As he left, other now familiar voices floated up to me again.

" . . . humanitarian purposes."

"Impossible, I tell you. Impossible."

My benefactor turned out to be a businessman from Zimbabwe heading overland for England. His wife had an amazing supply of disinfectants and gauze and a charming accent. When she finished cleaning the wound I asked her if she happened to have any suturing equipment.

"I'm sorry. I don't. But if I did you know I'd surely have a bash at it."

I knew she would and thanked her for her help. As it turned out, she and her husband were to unwittingly render me one more service before they left.

I noticed as they clambered down from the truck that the argument outside had stopped. We soon learned that the chief official had made arrangements with the couple for a ride to the next town. Within a few minutes they were gone. This meant that the man who had been arguing our case was now in charge. I assumed with relief that there would be no more obstacle to our crossing the border, but I hadn't reckoned on the transformation which the assumption of authority would make. Our erstwhile supporter now had second thoughts. The argument was resumed, this time with Dave Saguan, Lukanga's mission director, taking part. Dave had arrived providentially at Ishango just hours before the accident and was now doing his best to get medical help.

"If you let us through, we'll come right back just as soon as our man has been to the hospital. I give you my word."

"I don't know. I certainly would like to help you for humanitarian purposes, but there are eight of you on that truck. You are a Filipino; you've got a Dane, an American, a Canadian, and four from Zaïre with you. None of you have any documents, no visas, no passports, nothing. It can't be done."

His words had an air of finality about them, but, well versed in the free spirit of African debate, Dave brushed his objections aside as insignificant trifles and kept the discussion alive.

It was at this juncture that one of the Ugandan officials wandered by to see what was happening. He gave the assurance that we would be allowed into Uganda if we could get out of Zaïre. Whether it was his intervention or Dave's persuasion, I don't know, but before long we were on our way through the first of the border barriers. All told, there were five barriers to be crossed before we were on our own inside Uganda. Each of these necessitated lengthy explanations and arguments, and, in spite of the fact that we had set out at four o'clock in the afternoon, it was approaching midnight when Chuck finally pulled the truck to a stop in front of the hospital.

Messengers hurried off to the doctor's house at our arrival, but it was a good hour before he stumbled in, not quite awake. I was greatly relieved to learn from him that, although the recent war had diminished the stock of supplies in the hospital, they did have local anesthetic once again.

Unfortunately, the anesthetic had only a minimal effect, and I groaned as the doctor started to work. Immediately Chuck and Stefan appeared from around the corner in the hall, each holding a piece of cake.

"Great little hospital, this," said Chuck. "Best cake I've had in a long time. How's it going?"

I groaned again as the needle found another tender spot. Chuck apparently took it to be an encouraging sign. "Sounds as if you're going to pull through all right. I'd give you a bit of cake, but you'll have to wait. Doctor's orders."

From my position I couldn't see the doctor well enough to get confirmation of the statement, but at any rate, hunger was far from my mind. I just wanted to get things over with as quickly as possible. The doctor, for his part, appeared to have no objection whatsoever to the intruders in his operating room.

Time dragged on. Visitors kept wandering in and out of the room. Dave's visits were short. He kept his distance and avoided looking directly at the procedure. Stefan had hurried out shortly after first coming in, looking distinctly uncomfortable, and when he did come back in briefly to check on progress, the piece of cake was conspicuously absent. Chuck, on the other hand, took everything in with deep interest, keeping up a steady and spirited conversation and stepping out only to replenish his supply of cake. The nurse, who appeared somewhat nonplussed by his attitude, made only infrequent appearances at the operating table, evidently spending most of her time taking care of my colleagues. She looked pointedly at Chuck a few times, but he cheerfully ignored her and kept up the conversation. I was glad he did. I very much needed the distraction and he knew it.

At length the doctor put the last stitch in place and stumbled from the room wordlessly. I'm not certain that he ever was quite awake during the whole procedure, but he ap-

THE HUMANITARIAN BORDER GUARD 21

peared accustomed to working under such conditions and did a good job.

We made it back to the border in the early morning hours. This time the gates opened without argument just as quickly as the guards could be found. At the last barrier, going into Zaïre territory once again, we found our official still at his post, if not quite awake. He recognized us at once, and with a magnanimous gesture, waved us on. I could barely hear his voice as we drove on through, but three words were unmistakable.

" . . . for humanitarian purposes."

A Backward Glance

It all depends on your point of view, I suppose. The doctors told me I was lucky that the hippo bit me where it did. They said it would have caused a lot more damage elsewhere. I don't know. I found the whole thing rather embarrassing. It was also very hard to sit. I spent most of my time face down in bed.

Things weren't all bad, though. The recovery process went along very smoothly. I received a lot of company and had some very pleasant visits. I had a lot of time for thinking. Invariably, my thoughts often went back to the time we first came to Zaïre.

We had finally left for the mission field late in September 1978. From the plane, we watched excitedly as the last few glimpses of North America rapidly disappeared from view. Within a few short hours, we would be landing in Europe. After months of waiting, things were happening—happening fast.

Perhaps it was this sensation of speed, or perhaps, the ill-founded optimism of inexperience. But as we crossed the bleak Atlantic Ocean, we developed the notion that we would be arriving almost immediately at Lukanga in Africa. We should have known better, of course. Already, there had been a few little signs.

Several weeks earlier, I had been obliged to make an

emergency trip to Ottawa to take care of last-minute visa problems. Everything had worked out, but it could have meant a delay of months. Then, just hours before our flight, there had been an emergency phone call to headquarters to find out why our tickets hadn't arrived. It had been another near thing, but again, it had worked out. The airlines had been most cooperative, and it looked like smooth sailing the rest of the way. Our tickets indicated a day's layover in Brussels and then on without delay to Kigali and Gisenyi, Rwanda. From there, we knew, it was only a short drive across the border into Zaïre and then on up to Lukanga. All told, we figured, we should be arriving within forty-eight hours. Our experience with the Bauers, friends from our missionary training program, should have warned us otherwise.

We had first met the Bauers several months earlier at Missions Institute, a church-sponsored missionary training program, and were delighted to meet them again at the airport in Montreal. We had the same flight to Brussels. They too were bound for Zaïre, but would be stopping in Europe first for language study. We met up again after clearing customs in Brussels.

"Here, let me help you with those bags. Looks like you've got about all you can handle." It was Eldon Bauer offering to help, and he was guilty of a gross understatement. We had more than we could handle, and we'd been wondering how we would get it all to the platform where we could catch the train into town. Already, we had strapped a few small items to our children and were struggling to carry the rest to the train platform, around a corner, and down a flight of stairs from the customs. Mrs. Bauer stayed to guard their things until ours were taken to the waiting train. With Eldon's help, we soon arrived at the open door of the train, but no sooner had we stepped aboard than there was a soft buzz and a whir, and the train doors slid shut behind us.

"Hey, wait! I'm not going anywhere!" Eldon yelled frantically.

But no one heard him. We pushed and pulled at the doors, but there was no moving them. Fifteen minutes later an official sauntered by to check the tickets, but by then it was too late.

Eldon looked at us and we looked at Eldon. Like it or not he was going with us to downtown Brussels, while his wife waited at customs with the luggage.

It was close to two hours before Eldon could get a train back to the airport and customs. The ticket collector wanted him to pay for his ride, and none of us had any Belgian money. We were riding courtesy of the airlines, but the ticket collector figured Eldon was a stowaway. After long and tedious explanations, they finally let him ride back, where he found his wife still waiting patiently by their luggage.

The flight from Brussels the following evening went well, and before we knew it, we were landing on the grass strip at Gisenyi in Rwanda. The local priest, a man named François, who doubled as airport manager, graciously consented to drive us into town. Chickens, goats, and children fled before us as we bounced along the rutted road, horn tooting and dust flying.

François pulled to a stop at the tiny Regina Hotel. He unloaded our luggage and, with a wave of his hand, our newly found friend backed up and drove off. As we watched him leave, we couldn't help but feel lost and alone on this vast continent of Africa. It was an overpowering feeling of anonymity, as if no one in all that great expanse of land had any inkling that we were there. It was an eery feeling and the feeling turned out to be perfectly true. No one did know we were there. Due to a mix-up in dates, we were not expected. It was two days before I found the church headquarters—four miles and a border away.

"Hello," I said, arriving at the mission headquarters. "I'm the new missionary for Lukanga. Could you tell me what arrangements have been made to get us up that way?"

Still weak from a recent illness, Pastor Seraya welcomed me graciously to Zaïre. He assured me in his soft-spoken way that he could certainly tell me what arrangements had been made. None.

"Is there any way the principal at Lukanga could be contacted and told that we are here?"

"Yes, he's on the radio every morning at 6:30. We'll pass on your message."

"Fine. I'll be back tomorrow morning and see what is happening," I responded.

I was back the next morning around ten. I learned that the local church headquarters had a radio, all right, but it could only be operated by a twelve-volt battery. They had a twelve-volt battery, but it was in their Land Rover. No one seemed quite sure where that was. "But it'll be back today," the pastor said, and surprisingly enough, it was. When I went back the next day, contact with Lukanga had been made, and the principal was on his way.

The 190-mile trip from Gisenyi to Lukanga is very neatly divided into two parts by a large game park through which one must drive. Darkness had fallen as we neared this area, and the principal, Tim Korson, assured us that lions, jackals, hyenas, and elephants were everywhere. With just a little imagination, we could see cold, staring eyes reflecting the light from our headlights as we passed slowly along. I felt Diane beside me shiver, and she pulled the children a little closer.

We hadn't gone far through this area when suddenly one of the rear tires went flat. A quick search of the vehicle revealed no trace of a jack, so we were forced to improvise. There could have been no better introduction to travel in Africa. Vehicles here are kept together by string, wire, and inner tubing. Thick branches commonly serve to replace or repair broken springs and, as in our case, to take the place of jacks. The axle was propped up on a log, and we set to work digging out the dirt under the tire with a screwdriver. Tim looked over and commented wryly, "It's amazing what you can do when you have the proper tools!"

While all of this was going on, Diane kept a sharp eye out for danger. We had heard some hair-raising tales about lions and leopards, and when you're working in the dark, that sort of thing can't help but make you nervous. Some instinct told us that danger was in the air and, as events were soon to demonstrate, the instinct was correct. Danger, indeed, was close at hand and coming ever closer.

I was propped up on one elbow under the car, digging away, when suddenly, bright headlights illuminated my working space. A huge truck rolled up and came to a stop some fifteen feet away. The driver climbed down and casually sauntered over to see if he could help. It would have been of more help had he stayed in the truck. We were on a downhill slope, and his truck immediately began to roll toward us. There was no time to do anything and certainly no way to get out from where I was, so I prepared for the worst and braced for the impact. It never came. Just feet away from disaster, the brakes on that giant truck squealed, and it jerked to a stop. A passenger had reached over with his foot and stepped on the brake.

I scrambled out as quickly as I could and watched as Tim escorted our erstwhile Good Samaritan back to his truck. The man, apparently offended at our refusal of his help, roared off in a great cloud of dust, missing the car by inches. We breathed a sigh of relief and thanked God for His protection. As we were rapidly learning, you can always count on problems in this country, but what keeps it interesting is that you never know just what form they are going to take.

The next day was almost gone before Tim pointed out the

shining metal roofs far up the distant valley that was soon to be home.

Friday evening at five o'clock we pulled up to our new house. My diary for the day simply states, "Finally, we are here." Yes, finally, we had arrived. There could be no turning back. Our missionary career had begun.

As I looked up at the setting sun that evening, it struck me as particularly appropriate that our arrival at Lukanga so nearly coincided with the arrival of the Sabbath, the Lord's day. We were here on His business, and it was just one more reminder that from now on, our time was His.

Early Days of Mission Life

Our early days at Lukanga, as could be expected, were busy ones. We spent them unpacking, exploring our new surroundings, and trying to settle into the routine of life on the mission compound. The unpacking and the exploring went well, as there was little to unpack and much to explore, but the settling into a routine was much more complicated for, as we soon discovered, there is very little about life in this corner of the mission field which is routine. This was brought home to me forcibly by an incident in the early days of November.

Tim Korson and I were traveling on school business. Our itinerary brought us to the Virunga National Park, where we elected to spend the night. Painfully aware of the cost of food in that isolated area, we had brought along a large supply of bananas to tide us over. Some of these had become overripe, and we threw them into the wastebasket of the room where we were staying. Before going to sleep I determined to dispose of those bananas elsewhere at the dawn's first light. But by the dawn's first breaking I had greater problems than overripe bananas on my mind.

We were miles from civilization, and the only night sounds were the distant calls of wild animals. The air was somewhat odoriferous from the bananas in the wastebasket. We were sleeping peacefully when we were suddenly awakened just before daylight by a series of mild earth tremors.

"What's that, Tim?" I queried.

"Nothing to be worried about. Just a bit of an earthquake," he said, quite calmly. "Happens all the time around here. Has to do with all the volcanoes."

Virunga National Park is famous for its volcanoes, many of which are active. The word *virunga* itself means "volcanoes," and tourists frequently climb one of the larger ones for the privilege of looking down into its red-hot cauldron. I knew that earthquakes and volcanic activity are often associated with one another and was inclined to agree with Tim. But the tremors didn't stop.

"That other noise, Tim, that snorting. What's that?" I asked.

Tim jumped bolt upright in bed. "Hey, that's no earthquake! That's an elephant!"

We dressed hastily and dashed outside. It was indeed an elephant. He stood not thirty feet from our cabin enjoying his breakfast leisurely at a drive-in—a pickup truck parked at the cabin next to ours. Under a tarp in the back of the pickup were large baskets filled with vegetables. As we watched, the elephant reached under the tarp with his trunk, pulled out a basket of potatoes, and stuffed the potatoes into his mouth, then reached in again, this time coming up with a basket of carrots. These he chewed appreciatively, evidently pleased to find his breakfast packaged in such convenient bite-sized portions.

We stood there and admired the spectacle for some time, even taking a few pictures, until it suddenly occurred to us that the man in the adjoining cabin who was unknowingly supplying this mammoth breakfast might have an interest in what was going on. Keeping a wary eye on the elephant, I ran over and banged on his door.

He emerged sleepily. "Wha-what do you want?" he asked.

I jerked a thumb in the direction of his truck. "Elephant," I said.

"Wha-what?" He looked with heavy-lidded eyes toward his truck. The elephant was a scant fifteen feet away, completely filling the horizon. Only the truck was separating us. It rocked back and forth violently as the elephant continued to empty the pickup's contents. The enormous beast towered above us, grunting happily, its pungent odor rankling in my nostrils. All of my senses screamed, "ELEPHANT!" but my neighbor had not reacted at all. He simply stood there, the vacuous look of sleep still heavy in his eyes.

"Elephant!" I yelled it this time. "He's taking your food!"

This brought a reaction. The man's eyes widened suddenly, his mouth dropped open, and he uttered a feeble but horrified cry of recognition. "Elephant!" He ran to the truck, shouting and waving his arms. Surprised, the elephant backed away, and the man leaped into the cab, gunned the motor, and lurched off.

This is when I made my mistake. While Tim drove his own vehicle safely out of reach, I wandered innocently back to the cabin. With the excitement over, I had hopes of getting just a little more sleep before we set out on the road again. However, the elephant had other ideas.

Upset at having the serving dishes pulled away before he had finished eating, the elephant looked around for more. As he passed near our cabin, the unmistakable odor of bananas came wafting through the air. He gave a snort and headed for the door. I had left it open, expecting Tim back at any minute, but when I heard the footsteps approaching I knew they were not Tim's, and I knew there'd be no more sleep that morning.

The cabin was partially divided by an inner wall into two halves. I was in one, flat against the far wall, trying to look as inconspicuous as possible. The wastebasket with the bananas was in the other. The elephant was at the door, blocking my only exit and trying hard to join me. No doubt he could see the bananas clearly from where he stood, and he could certainly smell them, but he couldn't quite reach them. He stretched out his trunk and waved it, first at me and then at the bananas. It seemed for all the world as if he were ordering me to fetch those bananas for him and to be quick about it. I would have been more than happy to oblige, for an elephant's orders are not to be taken lightly, but it was out of the question. It would have meant coming within range of that swinging trunk and those fearsome tusks, and that was plainly a task for stouter hearts than mine.

It looked for a while that he might actually succeed in breaking in. He put his massive head down, and the cabin frame shuddered as he pushed and strained. But the walls were solid and the opening small. At last he seemed to realize that it wasn't to be. He turned away in disgust and started to leave. I shakily unpeeled myself from the wall and belatedly shut the door with a sigh of relief. It was premature. My troubles weren't over yet.

The elephant spotted a glass of water on the windowsill by the bed. The fact that it was behind a closed window with metal bars seemed not to deter him in the least. He leaned his great forehead against the frame and pushed. This time his efforts were rewarded. The bars bent and the windowpane exploded at once into a hundred tiny shards of glass. His long trunk snaked through the bars and curled triumphantly around the glass of water. As he attempted to pull it back through the bars, it slipped and fell with a crash to the floor. Disaster was piling on disaster and the water ran in rivulets around the broken bits of debris.

This time, the elephant apparently had had enough. He turned and walked straight to a nearby tree several inches in diameter. Ripping it from the ground, he disdainfully threw it aside. I think he was working out his frustrations.

To prevent any further problems, I took the basket with the bananas and threw it to him. He immediately picked up and swallowed it whole, bananas, basket, and all. What happened after that I don't know. Tim and I took advantage of the lull in the action to clean up all the mess, throw our stuff into the car, and drive off.

They say an elephant never forgets. I don't know whether this is true or not, but two years later I spent the night with my family at the same cabin in the same park. At dawn, Danny and Heather went to the window and excitedly announced, "Daddy, there's an elephant out there."

As I had two years earlier, I pulled on my clothes hastily and dashed outside. There he was again, larger than life. For several minutes we stood and stared at one another, neither of us moving in the flat gray light of the early morning. Then, with a look of condescension, he walked a short distance away and casually broke a small tree in half. It had been growing directly in front of the door where we had had our previous encounter. He looked back over his shoulder to where I was standing, opened his mouth in what appeared to be a wide grin, and winked, at least so it seemed to me. Then he nonchalantly turned and walked away.

The Trees of Lukanga Mission

I was cheating. I had driven up the valley to Rwese to take care of business at the field headquarters and should have driven right back down to school. There was work piling up in the office, a math lesson to be prepared, and a psychology lesson after that. But as I started down the road, I knew at once that they would have to wait. It was one of those beautiful Kivu days when the sun shines warm and the clouds have fled before the wind. Below me in the emerald green valley which was home, tin roofs sparkled like jewels in the bright sun. I pulled to a stop and climbed out. The wind buffeted me as I stepped around the car, and off the road. I lay down on the coarse grass where I entered a world of incredible calm.

Beyond me, the broad flat leaves of a banana grove snapped violently to and fro in the fierce wind, but here the air was warm and still. Insects buzzed through the grasses and a goat grazed contentedly. I could see the narrow footpath as it came out past the banana trees and wandered on down until at last it reached the road. I could see the square little thatched-roof huts and their round thatched-roof kitchens beside them, smoke flowing down the valley in a long flat stream before the wind. I could see, too, the little brook by the path as it rushed toward the school.

It was a sight which I have seen many times but which has

never failed to inspire me. Somehow it seems that for a moment I have the rare privilege of stepping aside and watching as life flows past all around me. At times, when I am in a philosophical mood, I think of how life is rushing me along, down through unnamed and unknown valleys. But this day was too beautiful for philosophy and too bright for dark thoughts. I reveled in the peace I felt, at one with God and His universe. A few more golden minutes passed before I reluctantly rose and walked back to the car and the world of wind and work.

As I neared Lukanga, the trees on the hill behind the school caught my attention. Planted only a few years ago, they were growing fast and made an impressive sight as they waved in the wind. Looking at them, I immediately thought of Masanga.

Masanga has worked at Lukanga for years and has planted just about everywhere and worked at just about everything. He had planted all those trees up on the hill. A typical Nande, he is slender and short and faces life with the gentle acceptance which is so characteristic of these people. He has seen some remarkable changes in his lifetime, and this may account for the look of perpetual astonishment on his face.

Masanga was once considered to be a highly educated man. Twenty-five years ago his grade 9 education earned him a job teaching school. Several of his former students now occupy prominent positions throughout the country. But time brings change, and as the years went by, Masanga found himself rapidly losing ground. All around him young people were finishing ten, eleven, and, increasingly, twelve years of schooling. New rules came into effect, and before long he was no longer allowed to teach.

For a while, Masanga worked at a variety of jobs around the school and then, undaunted by age, he enrolled as a student in the pastoral training school. When upon finishing the one-year course, he found himself still without a job, he started planting trees on a contract basis here at the school. This is the job he was doing when I first met him. He greeted me in the style so typical of the Nande people and so amusing to others.

"What news?"

To this, I had already learned that the expected answer is "No news." But the greeting wasn't over yet. He continued. "Are you awake?" To this as well, I had already learned the response.

"Yes, friend, I am awake."

The final words of the greeting were also automatic and can only be translated by the English slang, "OK, hang in there."

After this exchange, I could see that Masanga had something else to say. He held a bundle of young eucalyptus trees over one shoulder and an outsized hoe over the other. He set them down and looked at me expectantly.

I didn't realize in those early days that the surprised look he wore was a permanent fixture and immediately assumed that something I had said must have startled him. Perhaps it was the greeting. The words were somewhat complicated, and I was forever getting them wrong. I had several times informed people that in fact I was not awake, and they had always seemed only too inclined to believe me. I decided to switch back to French and try to get a conversation started with him.

"You planting those trees somewhere?" It was a rather weak opening, but he seized on it eagerly. There was no more hesitation. Pointing to the hillside where he was planting, he came right to the point.

"One can plant trees only after the rain. That is very cold work, standing barefoot in the mud. I saw you wearing some fine boots the other day. Do you suppose I could buy them from you when you leave?"

I looked at him in surprise. "Why, friend, what good does it do to talk of things so far away? I'll be here for another six years, maybe nine, and maybe more. Do you think I can remember a promise so far in the future?"

Now it was his turn to be surprised. The habitual look on his face intensified, giving the impression of a man whose astonishment could know no greater depths. He turned slowly and pointed again to the hillside where, already, tiny eucalyptus trees were bowing before the gentle breeze.

"Do you see those trees which I have planted? Some of them have been growing now for six months, more if you count the time they were in the seedbed at my home before I transplanted them. They will grow quickly. In five years they will be thirty feet tall. In eight years, or maybe ten, the school will start cutting them for firewood. I will get a certain amount of money from the school for each tree they use, but I won't get paid until the trees are cut. I will be paid for today's work in ten years."

The expressions on our faces must have looked very similar at that moment, for I was astonished. There was no telling what would happen in ten years or who would be in charge of the school, but a promise had been made and Masanga believed it.

I learned a lot about planning ahead that day; I learned a lot about trust. They were lessons I hope I don't forget. A year later, when I became principal, one of my first jobs was to count the trees growing on the hill and to see that Masanga was paid in full. No man should have to wait ten years for his wages. And I went a step further. I gave him my boots.

A Sermon Goes Wrong

I am always glad for an invitation to preach in one of the villages near Lukanga. It's one of the privileges which come with being a missionary, and one I don't take lightly. Because most of these villages are rather hard to reach, they don't get many visitors. When I pull up to the church on my motorcycle, Bible and hymnbook in a backpack, the entire membership rushes out to greet me. They treat me like royalty. I have preached at dozens of these churches, but one of my favorite churches is at Kakohwa, near Mageria. It's because of Mulyango.

Mulyango is one of the leading members of the Kakohwa church. I have yet to ascertain his official function; he is neither pastor, nor elder, nor deacon; yet when I come he takes me under his wing. I'll never forget a visit I made there early last year.

"What news, Mr. Prouty?"

"No news today, Mulyango."

"Fine, fine." He paused, as if to think, although I knew the words which must follow.

"Are you awake?"

"Yes, friend, I am awake."

Again he paused, as if searching for words, before completing the time-honored formula. "OK, hang in there."

"Mulyango, it looks as if you have a big crowd out today.

Two hundred, maybe? What do you think?" I asked, looking at the crowd in the church.

"Two hundred it is," came the response. This time there was no pause, for Mulyango was always totally in agreement with anything I might have to say. It was perhaps a weakness in my character that I found this trait so agreeable.

He looked at me with shining eyes, indicating with every fiber of his being his intense pleasure at my visit. "Perhaps you'd like to sit in one of these chairs?" The church members were studying the week's Scripture lesson in little groups scattered about on the church lawn, but two chairs had been found somewhere, one for him and one for me.

"If you don't mind, Mulyango, perhaps we could pull our chairs back by this tree. It's terribly hot out in the sun."

"Far too hot," he replied immediately, "far too hot."

We picked up our chairs and placed them under the tree. It was hard to balance them, as the back legs kept sinking into the soft sod, and there was a continual risk of falling over backward. It would have been much easier just to sit on the grass. But the chairs had been provided, and it would have been in bad form to refuse them.

I decided to put these few minutes left before the church service to good use. I had been studying the Nande language for quite some time by this point and had decided to use it for my sermon. I would be reading from a prepared text but was still a bit uncertain as to the pronunciation of some of the words. Leaning over precariously in my chair, I read out a few of them to Mulyango.

"How do they sound? Do I have them right?"

"Perfect," came the immediate assurance, "absolutely perfect."

The lesson study came to a close, and slowly the little study groups outside drifted into the church. I stepped around with the others taking part in the service to a little

A SERMON GOES WRONG 39

anteroom for last-minute instructions. As the song leader led the congregation in singing "Praise God From Whom All Blessings Flow," we took our places on the platform. I knew at once that I was in trouble.

Every seat in the church was filled. All along the walls people were standing, blocking out the light from the windows. It was so dark in the church that I could hardly recognize the faces of people I knew. There was no way I would ever be able to read my notes, and I knew I could never give the sermon by heart.

We worked our way through the offerings and the Bible reading and the musical selections. As time passed, I felt a faint hope stirring within me. My eyes were gradually adjusting to the darkness. By turning my notes at an angle, perhaps I would be able to catch enough light to get by.

My turn came to speak. Mulyango, sitting to one side, smiled at me encouragingly. I took a deep breath and started in.

It was slow going. The little light there was kept shifting, and my notes became more and more difficult to read. I began stumbling over words, pausing, stopping, and starting again.

As I struggled on, the congregation was quiet and polite. I looked around at the few faces I could still see. There were no signs of amusement, only a calm serenity and, evidently, a deep interest in what I was saying. The Nande's are a wonderful people. Their patience is legendary.

Late in the sermon, I came to a passage which dealt with Joshua presenting his family before the Lord. The word for *family* in the Nande language, *kitunga*, is spelled exactly the same as the word for *basket*, although there is a difference in pronunciation. Just before the sermon I had asked Mulyango for the right pronunciation and had been assured that mine was "right, absolutely right."

I launched into the subject of Joshua's integrity. "Nothing in this world, neither gold nor silver, neither honor nor fame nor friends—" I paused for effect and out of the corner of my eye could see Mulyango beaming up at me. I continued with emphasis. "Nothing in this world is more important than a Christian basket."

I had gotten it wrong and I knew it. But there was nothing I could do. The accumulation of errors, capped by this crowning and colossal blunder, was more than even these dear people could bear and the laughter was loud and long. The sermon came mercifully to a close shortly after that point.

I sought out my friend, Mulyango, immediately after the service.

"I guess I should never have tackled it in Nande," I said ruefully. "I really must have sounded like an idiot."

He looked at me happily. "Right you are," he said, "absolutely right."

The Family on Safari

Usually when I visit the churches down by the lake I leave my family behind. This is not so much out of a desire for solitude as it is out of necessity. The rutted track which winds through the hill country surrounding the lake fades into nothingness long before the lake can be seen. From that point forward, it's on by foot through the forest and down the steep slope to the park lands which border the lake.

It's an area of deep gullies and beautiful panoramas. Mountain gorillas live in the hills, along with chimpanzees, monkeys, and bush babies. The erosion-scarred valleys abound with colorful varieties of birds. Antelope, lions, and elephants roam the low-lying land near the lake. There is quite possibly no other place like it on earth for beauty and excitement, but it's no place for a family excursion.

In early August of 1980, the church members from Kitolu sent a messenger to invite me to their village.

"Lwatumba," I asked the messenger, "what is the road like these days?"

"Road?" he repeated doubtfully, as if trying to remember whether or not there actually was a road. "Ah, the road. It will be no problem at all." This was small consolation. The villagers always tend to minimize the problems with the road. As long as the major bridges are in place and one can get through on foot, there is "no problem."

I only had a few days to prepare for the outing, and at the last minute there was a change in plans. Diane decided that she and the children should come along. I was glad for the company but wasn't at all convinced that it was for the best.

"Are you sure you can make it? There'll be a long walk and no hot bath waiting when you get there."

She was offended. "Who is it who cooks your meals on a wood stove every day? Who feeds the family without so much as the use of a refrigerator? Who washes the clothes in a laundry tub?"

I had the strong feeling that she was referring to herself. If so, then what she was saying was true. She had made some remarkable adaptations to mission life, and if she felt she was up to the trip, I was in no position to argue. Anyway, I rather suspected that two events back in Canada had influenced her decision to come along. On August 7, my sister, Joy, was being married. On August 10, it was my brother, Bill's, turn. We had hoped to be there for these events, but a continent and an ocean had proven to be formidable obstacles. It hadn't worked out. The safari to Kitolu, from August 8 to 10, would be in way of compensation.

We felt a curious sort of quiet elation as we loaded our back packs and equipment into the Land Rover. I looked at Diane and she looked at me. It didn't take a crystal ball to read one another's thoughts. We were leaving the mundane world of the classroom and the kitchen behind. At last we were going to be on a safari, if only for a weekend.

We set out in high spirits. For an hour, the road climbed steadily through an increasingly wild region we had never visited before. Rocky outcrops rose above us to the right, and deep valleys fell away to the left. Spindly moss-covered trees and scrub brush gradually replaced the tall eucalyptus as we continued climbing. Then, two hours into the journey and around a sharp bend in the road, we came to the end of the ride.

"What are all those children doing in the road?" Diane's question was a good one, and for a moment I wasn't sure. Then it dawned on me.
"They're playing soccer; this is their field."
"Well, where does the road go from here?"
A good question. The road didn't go anywhere from there. It just seemed to die out somewhere behind the goalposts. We turned around and looked for a better place to park. From here on we would be walking.

Two hours down the trail, the valley of the Semliki River suddenly came into view. The Ruwenzoris, a mountain group sometimes called the Mountains of the Moon, reached far into the clear blue sky, white snow reflecting the bright sunshine with dazzling brilliance from the highest peaks. From this vantage point we could also see our destination, a tiny village on a distant hill.

I looked at Diane. She was breathing hard from the unaccustomed exertion. "Think you'll make it?"

She stopped to catch her breath before answering. "Doesn't look much farther to me. How far away is that hill? Five kilometers? I'll make it."

Just ahead of us, Heather and Danny were skipping merrily along, exploring every nook and cranny. They were enjoying themselves immensely and looked fresher than when we had started. I started down the path after them.

"Hey! Wait a minute!" It was Diane calling. I looked back. She was sitting on a rock by the side of the path. Her words came in short bursts. "Let's wait here—half an hour—give the kids—chance to rest."

So we rested.

When we got moving along again, the distant hill seemed to be receding before us. An hour, and then two, and it seemed almost as far away as ever.

"You don't think—that hill—is moving—do you, Bob?"

I was tempted to think so myself, but I said nothing and we kept on going. Only the beautiful scenery kept us moving. When we finally came to within a stone's throw of our goal, we found that a great chasm separated us from the village. The unexpected detour cost us another hour and three more kilometers.

We seriously wondered for a while whether we would make it, but make it we did, just as the last slanting rays of the sun tinted the distant snows a glowing pink and the dark shadows of the valley rushed up to meet us. Make it we did, with Heather and Danny running ahead over the last rise and down the last slope, Diane and me dragging along behind.

The village burst into joyous commotion at our approach, the women clapping and dancing and singing all around us. A spokesman stepped forward and welcomed us. It so happened that we were the first missionaries to visit since 1951! At this news, we exchanged weary glances. We were both born in 1951. They had been waiting a long time.

I quickly pitched the tent in the gathering dusk, as Diane soaked her feet blissfully in a bucket of hot water. She looked at me thoughtfully. "You said I wouldn't get a hot bath."

"The villagers are kind," I answered.

She continued. "Just think, at this very moment, back in Canada, they're probably halfway through the rehearsals for Bill's wedding."

"Wish you were there?" I asked.

"Yes, of course I do." She looked around her at the village scene, the distant mountains, and the dark valley. "Of course I do," she repeated, "but I wouldn't trade this for anything in the world."

What's in a Name?

Look on any map of Africa and you will find the Semliki River. It flows between Lake Edward and Lake Albert. It's a big river, full of fish and full of hippos, as I can personally testify. That's why its name is somewhat surprising. *Semliki* means "There is nothing in there." With the marvelous economy of words common to the Bantu languages, a whole sentence is condensed into those seven letters. The first two letters denote the negative, the *m* means "inside," the *li* is the verb "to be," and *ki* means "thing." One of the early European explorers, unfamiliar with the language but showing greater sensitivity than those who named the two lakes, wanted to find the local name for the river and addressed himself to someone standing nearby. His intentions were laudable but he made a slight error. The river's name is Kalemba.

The person by the river had a bag slung over his shoulder. Not understanding the language which the stranger was using, he assumed the explorer was asking what was in the bag. This would be considered polite among the Nande, just as we would consider it polite to inquire after someone's health. Hence the reply, "There's nothing in there."

The naming of the Semliki is typical of what happened throughout Africa as Europeans hastily tried to put a label on everything. Mount Kilimanjaro is another case in point.

The mountain's name is Njaro. *Kilima* is the Swahili word for mountain or hill. Lake Nyasa has recently changed names. It seemed redundant to the local people to be saying "Lake Lake." *Nyasa* means "lake." And so it goes throughout Africa. A lot of places are incorrectly named.

There is a big move these days to go back to the original names. This is undoubtedly as it should be. Names such as Stanleyville or Leopoldville, symbolic of the colonial powers, have no place in an independent country. Other names are changed for other reasons. Congo, for instance, was evocative of bloodshed and revolt and was changed to Zaïre because the government hoped to promote a more positive image. Besides, the Kongo are just one tribe in a country of hundreds of tribes.

These changes, if somewhat disconcerting to outsiders, make sense to us, and we have come to expect them. What those of us who are involved with schools find difficult is when a student decides to change his name. This happens often and can be very confusing. Paluku Tavalira, who came to my office one day, was a typical example.

"Sir, I've come to inform you that I want to change my name."

I looked at the student standing before me with interest, for he was a young man of above-average intelligence and good common sense. Many students change their names just for the pleasure of having something new, but I suspected that with Paluku Tavalira it was something more than that. I was curious to know his reasons, but first I had to encourage respect for the legal aspects of the situation. "You know we only allow name changes at the start of the school year. Changing your name at this date is highly irregular. I trust you realize that?"

He admitted the irregularity of his request but expressed hope that it would be granted anyway.

"And what is your new name to be?"

"Idem Tavalira. I found the other name in a book."

At this point it was tempting to jump to conclusions and assume the young man was simply indulging a ridiculous whim. It was easy enough to imagine where he had found the name *Idem*, and I certainly could see no logic behind his request. Still, something told me to check a little further. I have always had a lot of confidence in him, so I went ahead and asked the question I had been holding back until then.

"Just why is it you want to change your name?" I had more than one reason for questioning the change, for to anyone from these parts, his name, Paluku, is very meaningful. It immediately identified him not only as a Nande but as the oldest child in the family, just as Masika is used when the oldest child in the family is a girl. Among the Nande people, a rigid naming system is followed. As the second boy in my family I would have automatically been called Kambale were I a Nande. Indeed, at times I am called just that and I take it as a great honor.

Paluku picked up a piece of chalk from my desk and examined it thoughtfully as he searched for the proper words. "It's this way," he said at length, "I'm hoping to go to university in Kisangani next year, and there is a lot of trouble with tribalism. Some teachers give good grades to those from certain tribes and bad grades to those from others. If they see I'm a Paluku, they will know right off where I come from. There aren't many Nande teachers at the university, so we don't have many supporters in Kisangani. I might fail the year. But Idem and Tavalira would mean nothing to them. It would make things easier."

I had to admit he had a point. Tribalism is a serious problem. It would be reassuring to think it is dying out with the coming of Christianity, but that is not the case. Just two short years before we came to Lukanga, back in 1976, there was a riot here at the school. Windows were smashed; homes were broken into; lives were threatened. There were many causes that could be traced but underlying them all was tribalism.

That was seven years ago. Since then, there have been a few encouraging signs. Here at Lukanga there have been no flare-ups and generally, throughout the region, things have been calm. With people traveling more than ever before, there is a growing familiarity with other cultures and an increasing acceptance of other traditions. The generally higher level of education these days also helps make tribal differences seem less important. With each passing year at Lukanga, we see an increased level of intertribal mixing and friendships. But because the bonds of culture and language run deep, change comes slowly. Perhaps it is for the best. Where attempts have been made to change social patterns too abruptly, a rootless society has developed, with its attendant problems. Christianity should be and can be a powerful factor for removing the excesses of tribalism, but overall changes will come from within society itself, as cultural practices slowly adapt to a changing world. In the meantime, Paluku's problem is a real one.

He waited patiently while I thought about his question. I knew there could be only one answer. "Yes, Paluku, we'll let you make the change. You may see the secretary for the new documents."

Paluku smiled broadly. "Yes, sir, I understand. Thank you very much." He arranged the chalk neatly on my desk before continuing. "And please, sir, don't call me Paluku. Call me Idem." With that, he turned and was gone.

As I sit here writing, I'm holding my youngest son on my lap. It's a little awkward, but this is my turn to baby-sit. The question of names brings back fond memories of his birth a few short months ago. He was two days old and we still didn't have a name for him. It was a problem the Nande would never have known. Under their straightforward sys-

WHAT'S IN A NAME? 49

tem, he would have been called Kasereka. And for three days, Kasereka it was. We still couldn't agree on anything else. I was in favor of an original name; Diane wanted something more traditional.

"Diane, what do you think about Luke Angus? He'll never forget where he was born."

Diane countered with Douglas Grant.

I didn't like that one and we both started thinking again. She rejected my suggestion of Augustus after his month of birth as "too archaic." Robert Stewart Victor Prouty sounded good to her at first, but it too was rejected when she noticed the initials.

"Why are you always coming up with names that have a catch? Can't you suggest something ordinary?"

That's when I made my big move. "What do you think about Dorian Matthew?"

She was enthusiastic and for a moment it looked like we had a name. But my conscience was bothering me. Should I tell her or shouldn't I? I decided I should, though I have often wondered what she would have done if I hadn't.

"And just think, Diane," I added nonchalantly, "for short, we can call him Doormat."

We didn't call him Dorian Matthew, and we didn't call him Luke Angus or any of the dozen other little suggestions I made. We called him Jonathan Michael. Our Nande neighbors call him Kasereka, and I don't mind a bit. After all, what's in a name?

Kavis and the Nande Hymnal

Kavis was over at the house for his traditional Friday evening visit. The generator had long since been turned off, and the room was only dimly lit. Huge shadows danced on the wall behind him as he gestured his way animatedly through the conversation, moving impatiently from side to side in his chair, settling back, then lurching unexpectedly forward to drive home a point. As I looked at Kavis and at those leaping shadows, I couldn't help but think that this was one of those remarkable people who are truly larger than life.

Physically, there was not much to notice about him. Short enough to have earned the nickname Pygmy as a student, he was heavyset, with huge hands, only the sparkling eyes betraying his true nature. The nickname was ironic, for the year after obtaining his secondary school diploma, he went off to the forest for a year and worked among the Pygmies.

Just before leaving Lukanga, Kavis planted a hedge behind one of the houses, at the top of the hill which slopes down to the banana grove. It was a cyprus hedge and it grew well, but it had no sense of direction. It wandered in and out along the top of the hill, veering suddenly for no apparent reason and then, just as suddenly, resuming its former course. He revealed more of himself than he ever could have realized when he planted it, for he too had only a vague sense of direction. Some would have called him scatterbrained. He enjoyed work but could never stay with a project long enough to accomplish much. He was intelligent, but he only managed mediocre grades in school. He was overweight, and he tired easily.

His year with the Pygmies changed all that. Kavis developed gradually into a muscular young man with a serious side to go with his light-hearted nature. His sentences were still punctuated with laughter, but he had learned to think about the important things of life as well, and he had decided to become a pastor. Perhaps it is significant that by the end of the year, the hedge at the top of the slope had thickened so that its former meanderings were only faintly visible.

The work in the forest had been good training. The sheer physical effort of carving a living out of the jungle had been balanced with the invaluable experience of teaching school to a group of fresh recruits, unaccustomed to sitting on benches and with no sense of time. It had been a school of patience for Kavis. At sight of a monkey scampering across the little clearing where the school had been built, miniature bows and arrows appeared miraculously, and eighteen children disappeared just as miraculously off into the forest undergrowth. No school, indeed, no army on earth could have stopped them or brought them back before their quarry had been found. Only after the meat had been cooked and the last scraps devoured could the bell again be rung and classes resumed.

Kavis and a fellow pioneer, Masumbuko, built a little church in the forest. They soon found unexpected interest in their work by the world outside. An article, and then another, appeared in church magazines, and their photos appeared in every one of the magazines. It made little difference out in the forest, though, and Kavis worked on as before, until the time came when he could begin his pastoral training. It had been a rich experience for an orphan boy not yet twenty-one years old.

I had known Kavis from the time I first came to Zaïre, so it was not surprising that we had gotten into the habit of spending Friday evenings together. He was an entertaining personality and had a rich store of knowledge of local customs and traditions. He knew of my interest in languages, and on this evening, we had fallen naturally into a discussion of the Nande language.

"Kavis, what do you think of our Nande church hymnal?" I asked.

"It's good, very good, but—all the same—" His voice trailed off into silence.

I'd heard the expression before. No Nande would be so rude as to make an overtly negative statement. Disagreement is carefully couched in obfuscatory terms. Something which is bad is "good, but—"

"What's the problem with it, Kavis? Is it the translation? I know it was done thirty years ago."

He pushed forward in his chair, hands folded, elbows wide and resting on his knees. There was a moment's silence as he looked for the proper words. "Yes," he said at length, "it's the translation. We enjoy the hymnal very much, but we don't understand it all."

He reached for the hymnal I was holding and turned to number 40, a translation into Nande of the song, "Trust and Obey." "It's all very good except for verse two." He pointed. "Right there. 'Let the clouds gather.' Where did those clouds come from? And where did they go? Nobody knows, but we just sing right along." He read it to himself again and laughed aloud.

"Are there any other problems?" I have long been interested in translating, and the thought was beginning to jell in my mind that perhaps a revision of the hymnal would be a good start.

"Lots of mistakes, as our spelling system has changed since those days," he answered, "but the worst one is number 108. I always wondered about it when I was small, but I figured that it must be right. After all, the grown-ups all sang it."

As he struggled to suppress his amusement, I wondered what was in store. I turned quickly to number 108. I read, "Let the ladies bite the children." Kavis tried to sing it through but kept breaking down in laughter.

The translator's goal was commendable. The line should have read, "Let the ladies, men, and children." But while *abalume* means "men," *balume* means "bite," and from the way it was printed and from the way the melody went, there was no other way to sing it.

I looked over at Kavis again. He had long since abandoned any effort to be serious and was deep in laughter. His position on the chair was growing ever more precarious as each convulsive burst of laughter brought him closer to the edge. I would have tried to calm him down, but there is something very appealing and very contagious about a man in the throes of laughter and when at last the inevitable occurred and he pitched forward helplessly to the floor, it was several minutes before I could trust myself to speak. "Kavis," I finally managed, "what is it like when they sing it in church?"

He was beyond words. Every feature of his face had changed as wave after wave of laughter broke across its surface. He had heard the question but could only stammer, "Oh, oh," before dissolving completely. He didn't need to answer. I could well imagine the effect, and it was another five minutes before either of us was able to get on with the conversation.

For all the laughter, translation is a very serious problem throughout Africa, especially when one considers the abundance of tribal languages. Zaïre alone, by some counts, has over 500. Of these, Nande is one of the more important, spoken by over a million people. And yet, the first Nande translation of the Bible came out less than two years ago.

There are many problems involved in translation, but the biggest obstacle is money. Still, the problems can be surmounted and the work can be done.

"We need books, good books, in our own languages. And we will get them." Kavis became sober quickly.

"What about the money for printing the books, Kavis?"

"God will provide."

Coming from a young man who has spent a year with the Pygmies, living on nothing but faith, those words are not to be taken lightly.

Trivia

"Who was the only bachelor President of the United States?"
"James Buchanan."
"What year was he elected?"
"1856."
Robert Brock was at it again. He knew I loved trivia almost as much as he did and was forever trying to catch me.
"All right, Robert, here's one for you. Who was the first President of Canada?"
"Nice try, Bob, but I know better than that. You don't have presidents up there, just prime ministers, and the first one was MacDonald."
We were on our way to Butembo to make a few purchases for the school. Butembo is a town of over a hundred thousand inhabitants just twenty-five miles from Lukanga. In some respects it is only a village, for it has no electricity and little running water, but compared to most places it is thriving. You can find almost anything in the stores or in the stalls at the market if you look hard enough.
"I have a question for you, Robert."
"Shoot away, I'm ready. What would you like to know? John Tyler was the only president married in the White House. The edge of a quarter has one more groove than the edge of a dime." He laughed as he spoke.

"No, I'm serious this time," I said. "What do you think about school fees for next year?"

Robert is Lukanga's business manager. He is taller than average, broad-shouldered and slim. Except for the glasses, he looks more like a coach than an accountant. He handles everything from water pipes to workers' salaries. And, of course, the school fees. As usual, he had all the figures at the tip of his tongue.

"Cassava has gone from 80 zaïres to 200. Beans are at 450, up from 180 at the beginning of the year. Potatoes have tripled. Who knows where we'll be at this time next year?" He paused to do a little mental arithmetic before continuing.

"Sugar seems to have stabilized and flour may actually drop, but I still don't see how we can possibly set the fees any lower than twice what they were this year. Even at that, we may have to readjust halfway through."

I wasn't surprised. I had been hoping we could get by without an outright doubling of the fees but had known all along that there wasn't much chance. The economy is in bad shape, and I'm glad Robert deals with the money and not me. All the same, as bad as things are, I've seen it far worse.

It happened in December 1979, on Christmas Day, of all days. There was no forewarning, no rumors, nothing. Out of a clear blue sky, the announcement came over the radio that the country's paper money was no longer valid. Anywhere else, we would have refused to believe it, but some remarkable things happen at times and, preposterous as it seemed, we had to check it out. It turned out to be true. All five- and ten-zaïre bills were declared worthless. It was quite a shock.

Those who were first to hear the news didn't waste any time. A man in Butembo threw all of his money into his truck and rushed out into the countryside. He came in the early morning to an isolated village near Mageria where no

one had radios. The startled villagers awoke to the insistent blaring of the truck's horn and rushed out.
"What news?"
"No news, but I want to buy goats. I'll give you three hundred zaïres apiece."
Goats were selling for 100 zaïres at the time and word of the man's offer spread rapidly from hut to hut. "There's a madman here with a truck. He's giving 300 zaïres cash for goats, all goats: big ones, little ones, sick ones—doesn't matter. Hurry!"
Soon a crowd had formed as people tumbled from their huts and fell over one another in their rush to find their goats. Half an hour later, the truck, filled beyond belief with bleating goats, pulled out. We were still in bed here at Lukanga when the truck lurched past, heading for pastures unknown, and it was nearly noon before the poor villagers learned how they had been duped. By then it was too late. Like the businessman in Butembo who had just sold his truck, like the pickpocket who had just taken a wallet, like the teacher who had just been paid, they had lost all they had and there was no way to get it back.
The move had been made because of a crisis in the banks. Chronically low on cash, they had been increasingly unable to cash checks or allow withdrawals. As people lost confidence, more and more of them began keeping their money at home. It was a vicious circle and this was the result. Only money on account in the banks was exempt from the blow.
The morning's news brought only a faint glimmer of hope. Everyone would be allowed to trade up to one hundred zaïres of old money for new between December 27 and December 29. By five o'clock the next morning, I was at the bank. Or, to be more precise, near the bank. It was impossible to get right to the bank. A crowd of thousands had already arrived at the bank. Down the road at another bank it was the same story.

We waited for hours and at last the doors opened. Immediately, the crowd surged forward, only to be driven back by soldiers wielding billy sticks. A few people forced their way inside and the doors closed. This was repeated several times over the next few hours, each time with the situation and the crowds kept only tenuously under control by the billy sticks. Things didn't look very promising and when a sudden downpour of rain failed to diminish the crowds, we called it quits and went back home. It was just as well we did. Of the thousands and thousands standing outside those doors, hour after weary hour, barely a hundred were able to change their money before the three-day period ended.

The period which followed was a hard one. Businesses failed; people went hungry. At Lukanga, we carried on, but it wasn't easy. Food was in short supply and cash nonexistent. People traded the clothes off their back for something to eat.

That was four years ago. Things are better now. Inflation is running at around 100 percent and teachers' salaries are low, but things are better. The economy is in bad shape, and I'm glad Robert Brock deals with the money, but things are better.

Robert wasn't here back in those days. He came along three years later. Suddenly remembering this, I saw my chance and decided to try one more question on him.

"Hey, Robert, here's a bit of trivia I'll bet you don't know. What year did they change the money in Zaïre?"

He shot the answer back almost before the last words were out of my mouth. "1979. December. But from what I've heard it was far from trivial."

Yes, Robert, I guess you're right. A minor event in a far-off country to most people. Hardly a line in the financial news. An insignificant ripple on the world scene. But far from trivial for those of us who lived through it.

A Day to Forget

Impatiently, I flipped through the mail. It was summer. Trips to the post office in Butembo were rare, and a lot of mail had piled up. The school's box, number 180, serves not only the school but all of the surrounding villages, so a lot of the mail I was sorting was not even ours. I kept looking, carefully separating the envelopes and checking inside the wrappers of magazines. Yes, there it was. The little white slip. Half hidden between the pages of a trade journal which came faithfully from China. A little less care and I'd have missed it altogether.

Those little white slips in the mail always marked a high day for us, for they meant only one thing—a parcel too big for the box. Invariably, they were overlooked until the mail was more carefully sorted back in Lukanga, which meant another week's delay before the package could be collected. But this time I had forestalled all that with my careful search, and the name on the slip read Prouty. Silently congratulating myself, I hurried around to the wicket.

"You have a package for 180?"

The man behind the wicket made no reply; he took the slip in silence, turned and shuffled slowly from the room. Whether it was the perpetual licking of stamps that dampened his enthusiasm for conversation or whether it was just his nature, I have never determined. But that man behind the wicket almost never spoke. When he did, it was always with seeming resentment at the effort required. His few words were carefully rationed as if he were trying to keep within a daily quota.

As he disappeared from view, I felt the same nervous strain of anticipation I always do when waiting for a parcel from home. The strain is compounded by the knowledge that packages can disappear in that little back room and not emerge again for months, so when after several minutes he came out carrying a big package, I relaxed. I could recognize the handwriting; it was indeed from home.

The sight of a parcel from home put me in a lighter frame of mind, and while he thumbed through his registration book, I indulged in a game I had played with him before—I tried to get him to talk.

"Think it might rain?"

A shrug, noncommittal.

"Crops could use it."

A nod, seemingly in agreement.

I seemed to be doing a little better. I might get somewhere yet.

"You got much of a garden planted?"

Another shrug.

I had just about decided I wasn't going to succeed when he surprised me with a question of his own. "Got the school stamp?"

I had forgotten this part of the routine. To retrieve packages which come to the school address, the required procedure is to sign the registration book and stamp it with the school stamp. This country lives by the stamp; and all documents, report cards, and pay sheets must be stamped before becoming official.

I had early learned the importance of carrying the stamp with me and reached confidently into my briefcase. The ink pad was there; the stamp was not.

"Seems I left it back at school," I explained, chagrined. "I must have left it on my desk."

"No stamp, no package," he said. "You'll have to go and get it."

"But it's twenty-five miles back to Lukanga," I protested. "You know who I am. I'll stamp it next week when I come back."

"Sorry, can't do it. No stamp, no package."

He turned and shuffled off again, returning the package to the back room. When he returned, he was in no mood for further discussion. My remonstrances were greeted with silence and I returned to Lukanga empty-handed.

I kept the affair of the forgotten stamp strictly to myself. I had already developed quite a reputation for forgetfulness and could see no point in enhancing it any further. Besides, I thought to myself, there were others around who were just as bad, if not worse. Take Robert Brock, for instance. Why, he was forever having breakdowns with his car, and invariably he would have to trudge the long miles over the hills and back to Lukanga, having forgotten to bring along the very tool he needed. And then were was Stefan.

Stefan was a student missionary, out for eight months. His function was to teach the expatriate children. They were all on correspondence courses and he helped them along. He had, however, an unfortunate tendency to forget things. The children would take their exams, and he would forget to send them in for correction. He would forget which family he was eating with for the week. He would even forget which of us had borrowed his shortwave radio.

Several weeks after the post-office incident, I took Lukanga's volleyball team in my pickup to our sister school at Kanyatsi, twelve hours away. Stefan was coming along and, knowing his weakness, I went over his checklist with him in detail.

"Do you have your lunch, Stefan?"

"Oh, sure, I wouldn't forget that."

With his nineteen-year-old-appetite, one wouldn't think so, but surprisingly enough, he had managed to forget it on previous trips.

"What about your sleeping bag and your clothes? Do you have everything?"

The same nonchalant attitude. "Oh, sure, I've got everything."

Perhaps the memory of my recent experience at the post office was lurking somewhere in the back of my mind, or perhaps it was because of his lack of concern, but I couldn't resist giving a little extra advice at this point.

"All right, Stefan, but on a long trip like this one, it dosn't hurt to double check. You can be sure that I've gone over my lists carefully, and I think you should do the same."

Three hours into the trip, a tire went flat. I took out the jack and lug wrenches and quickly put on the spare. Ten minutes later we were on our way and at the next town, I had the flat repaired. I took advantage of the situation to reinforce my previous counsel.

"Imagine the time we would have lost, Stefan, if the tools had been forgotten." I didn't come right out and say so, but he knew I was referring to Robert, and I took his answering grunt to be a sign of agreement.

The trip went along without a hitch, and it was with a certain feeling of smugness that I headed the car into the final thirty-mile stretch before the town of Goma. That is a desolate piece of road, if ever there was one. Volcanoes rise on both sides and the landscape is pure science fiction, lava from recent eruptions covering the ground for miles in all directions. Only a few charred tree trunks break the monotony.

We were just over halfway through this section when the engine coughed and the truck stopped. I got out and made a pretense of lifting the hood, but our problem was clear. We were out of gas, and I soon realized I had forgotten to fill the jerry can before we left the mission.

Embarrassed, I looked over at Stefan. I had a pretty good idea of what he was thinking, but when he spoke, he gave no hint of it.

"What are you going to do?" he asked, as if I had any choice. There was only one thing to do, and I tried to sound as businesslike and efficient as possible under the circumstances as I explained to him.

"I'm going to get the jerry can out of the back of the truck and I'm going to hike in to Goma for some gas."

While he put down the hood, I went around to the rear of the truck. I came back half a minute later, empty-handed and red-faced. It wasn't my day. I had forgotten the jerry can too.

A Day to Remember

I like to think that for everyone, sooner or later, there comes a day when everything goes just right. My day came not long after the trip to Kanyatsi. After that experience, it couldn't have come at a better time. I have Carey Carscallen to thank for it.

The fact that both Carey's first name and his last start with the word *car* is surely more than coincidental, for he is in charge of all things mechanical at Lukanga, including the Lukanga Technical School, which he started up and built largely by himself. Four years ago, it was only a dream, but today it is a thriving school with a fine new building and nearly 200 students, and the future looks bright.

The man responsible for this remarkable development is tall and slim, with Nordic features. Like most of the missionaries at Lukanga, he is in his early 30s. He is a reserved man, soft-spoken but hard-working. A mark of his patience is that in the four years we have worked together, he has never commented to me about my lack of mechanical ability. This is more of an accomplishment than it may appear, for I am utterly useless when it comes to repairs and have had to call on him for help on numerous occasions. Everyone around Lukanga is aware of my shortcomings in this area, and most have found reason to comment on them at one time or another, with the notable exceptions of Carey and Wasukundi. Wasukundi's opinion changed abruptly on that one wonderful day which I shall never forget and which, in all probability, I shall never experience again.

The story actually begins a couple of months earlier, at six o'clock on an evening when our school generator refused to start. When the generator is working and when diesel fuel can be found, we get a few hours of electricity each evening. On this particular evening, with the generator balking, Carey was the man I went off to find. He came up to the generator room at once, with his box of tools and his flashlight. As there was no one else around, I got to hold the flashlight.

He worked away at length, testing the battery, the terminals and countless other bits and pieces of the generator, parts whose names I didn't know and of whose function I was totally ignorant. Time dragged by and in spite of his best efforts, all he could get when he turned the key was a loud clicking noise. I could see his frustration mounting and at length he lashed out with his foot at the box which holds (as he carefully explained it to me) the solenoid. It was the only time in all these years that I have seen him make such a gesture, and it did the trick. Another turn of the key and the machinery in that room leaped to life, like a repentant pet suddenly eager to please. Carey grinned in a guilty sort of way, and we gathered up the tools and went on back home. The little incident was to play a major role in my big day several months later.

The day started out simply enough, with a stiff wind and a strong sun. It was the kind of day I like the best. Even before I got to my office, I was able to enjoy a small triumph. As I walked up the steps in front of the classroom building, I noticed Wasukundi leaning over the lawn mower, a defeated look on his face. He is in charge of the daily workers and doubles as plumber and electrician. I could see that the lawn mower had him beat.

"What news, Wasukundi?"

"No news."

"Are you awake?" I asked the expected question in greeting.

"Yes, I'm awake, but this lawn mower—It won't start."

It was his first time using the lawn mower, as our regular man was absent, and I could see he wasn't used to it. I had already used it several times, and I saw the problem at once. The start lever on that mower is extremely delicate and must be placed just right to get things going.

"I'll start it for you, Wasukundi."

His face expressed his doubt more eloquently than words, but he stepped aside. I set the lever, pulled the cord, and it started with a roar. I showed him how to do it himself and went on my way. It was a minor accomplishment, but to a nonmechanic like myself, it set the tone for a day that went along without a hitch.

A little later in the morning, Chuck asked to borrow my motorcycle. He's a far better rider than I will ever be and has been around motorcycles all of his life. He performs wheelies as casually as if he were out for a stroll, and he's a capable mechanic. But he wasn't used to my bike and had trouble getting it started.

"I can get her going with one kick, Chuck," I offered.

He gave me the same dubious look I had seen minutes earlier. "You're on."

I pulled the choke just so, gave a vigorous kick, and shoved the choke back down. It purred like a cat.

"Nothing to it, Chuck, for us mechanics."

My crowning triumph was to come that evening, at six o'clock. I don't recall exactly why, but Wasukundi was still around. Usually, he goes home at three. At six, it's the night watchman, Mulenge, who starts up the generator. Mulenge had probably learned the little trick with the quick kick by this time, but Wasukundi hadn't, and as fate would have it, this was one of the nights it wouldn't start. Carey was gone, so Wasukundi called on one of the teachers at the technical school. He worked for half an hour or so, finally declared he would take the thing apart in the morning, and went on home. I have no doubt that he would have found the error in the morning and fixed the thing once and for all, for he was good, but he didn't know about the kick.

Wasukundi next called in one of the top students from the school, a young man who had developed quite a reputation for his troubleshooting skills. He got no further than his teacher and, deciding that a new battery was needed, he went off to look for one. Wasukundi was just stepping outside when I wandered by.

"What's up, Wasukundi?"

"Generator won't start." He described the problem, and when he mentioned the loud clicking sound, the experience of three months earlier came hazily into my mind.

"I'll start it for you if you like."

My early morning triumph had not been enough to overcome his long-held opinion of my skills, and for the third time that day, I saw the same scornful look. Again, he said nothing but simply stepped aside.

As I looked at that generator for the first time in months, I realized with a sinking feeling that I couldn't remember where I was supposed to direct my kick. I stalled for time as I tried to bring that hazy memory into sharper focus.

"Who've you called in?" I asked. He gave me the names.

"Good men," I nodded. "Good men, both of them. And you say they couldn't get it started?"

"Started?" He was emphatic in his denunciation of their skills. "They couldn't get a thing out of it. Just that clicking."

I said nothing but suddenly gave a violent kick to the side of the machine. Wasukundi looked rather startled but turned the key at my command. More clicking.

Just then, I noticed the little box jutting out. At once, it all came back to me. I knew I had it. That was the place to direct my kick.

"Watch this, Wasukundi." I gave a sharp kick and turned the key. The magic of three months earlier worked again, and that great machine hummed and vibrated with life. As I stepped out of the room, lights were glowing all over campus.

Just before I got out of range, I heard Wasukundi's voice behind me, talking to an onlooker in awed tones. "I can't believe it."

I couldn't believe it either, but it was true. It had been one of those days, and I quickened my step and whistled all the rest of the way home.

A Snake at the Baptism

Eighteen miles from the main road, Muhangi is situated deep in a large, spreading valley. Although much of the surrounding area has a temperate climate, the cool mountain breezes bypass Muhangi, and it is almost depressingly hot. The church is on a little knoll across from the town. Because there is no water, baptisms are held some distance away where a trickle of a stream runs along a small swamp. On Friday, the deacons dig a hole at the edge of the stream. One man bails and another man digs and after several hours they have a hole four feet deep and about four feet in diameter. When the bailing stops, the hole fills quickly with a dark, viscous liquid that seeps in from the swamp.

For some people, a wedding service brings tears to the eyes. For others, a funeral. For me, it's a baptism every time. I can never come away from one without a catch in my throat and a tear in my eye. It seems to me that of all the events a missionary is privileged to witness, none is more touching than a baptism. The public consecration of a life to the Lord is always an emotion-filled moment, but there is a unique feeling about an African baptism, a special throb of excitement in the air. Perhaps it is because the lives of these people are so hard and often so tragically short that their celebration of life seems so meaningful and is so often expressed.

One particular Sabbath as I pulled up on my motorcycle to where Sabbath School was being held, my clothes were already soaked with perspiration. It had not been the most comfortable of rides. Pastor Karambizi, the district pastor, had come with me. The ride was almost completely downhill and long before we arrived, I had slid forward onto the gas tank and he had assumed sole occupancy of the seat. Even after we stopped, he was clutching me so tightly around the waist that I had to invite him to let go and step down. I could hardly blame him. As district pastor, he had five or six churches under his care. Visits invariably required at least a half day's walk. To have arrived at such a breakneck speed must have been somewhat disconcerting, to say the least. We had covered the eighteen miles in just over an hour.

After greeting the church members, I walked over and took my place in one of the Sabbath School classes. Pastor Karambizi walked on by and gravely inspected the baptismal hole. It evidently met his approval, for he nodded his head, satisfied, and took his place on the bench beside me. He would be holding the baptism and I would do the preaching.

There is a little thicket of trees by the edge of that swamp. Its branches reach out over the spot where the pulpit had been placed. Along with two elders of the church, Pastor Karambizi and I stood under these branches after Sabbath School as we prepared for the following service. I noted a rustle just above my head and was startled to see a brilliant green snake slithering down through the branches.

"There's a snake in that tree, brother!" I whispered my message to the head elder as nonchalantly as possible, hoping to prevent a general panic. There was little danger. The elder glanced up casually in the direction I had indicated. "So there is," he said disinterestedly, and turned back to the immediate task of distributing the platform duties. He

A SNAKE AT THE BAPTISM 71

later posted a young boy with a stick by the tree as a concession to my fears. He may have been unconcerned—but I was not. My sermon was about the life of Peter, and I made him look heavenward as often as possible so I could get a look at that tree and see how things were coming. I just regretted I wasn't preaching about the Garden of Eden.

My fears turned out to be groundless. The snake made no further appearances, and I was able to finish my sermon without incident. I sat down with relief and watched as preparations were made for the baptism. Pastor Karambizi slipped behind the trees to change his clothes, and the entire congregation moved over and crowded around the hole. There was no song leader in evidence, but songs were sung with enthusiasm, everyone joining in. It was a little confusing at first. Several different church members began singing at the same time, each one with his own hymn. Each hymn attracted its group of supporters, and for a while there was spirited competition. Then, gradually, one by one, the less popular hymns were overwhelmed by the others and at last, somewhere part way through the second verse, everyone was together singing "The Crimson Wave." This was sung through in its entirety and then sung through again, the general feeling evidently being that this was a safer course than that of trying to get a consensus on a second song. As time passed, though, and the pastor still hadn't emerged from the trees, a few more hymns were sung. These were sung with as much enthusiasm as the former and this time there was unanimity from the beginning.

At length, the pastor emerged, the singing stopped, and the ceremony began. The candidates entered the hole and were baptized one by one, with the congregation softly singing "The Crimson Wave" as they emerged. They came out of the water, faces shining with joy, oblivious to the muddy water streaming from their clothes and forming puddles where they stood. They were giving their lives to the Lord, and they knew full well that there would be greater inconvenience than this.

At one point in the service, the pastor lost his footing and slipped. The candidate came up sputtering and coughing, and a roar of laughter went up. I looked about me with what I hoped was a reproving look, but I made no impression whatsoever. And with good reason. I was judging them according to my own Western standards, and these just didn't apply. As I quickly realized, they meant no lack of respect or reverence. They were totally involved in the service and reacted openly and without apology to whatever was happening.

I noticed not long after, a mother quietly wiping away tears of joy as a young man disappeared into the murky waters. Her son, perhaps, or a neighbor boy. How many years had she prayed for him? How many tears had she already shed? I brushed away a tear of my own and joined in the subdued singing as the last of the candidates was baptized. Then, standing in a hole filled with four feet of muck and slime, his white shirt filthy and his wide brow perspiring, the pastor stepped forward and addressed the crowd. He spoke as if he were standing behind the finest pulpit ever made and dressed in the best of robes. He called upon those present to make their stand for Christ. Tears flowed freely and decisions were made that will change lives forever. This is the power of the gospel, and this is Africa. I've thought many times how lucky I am to be a part of it all.

The last few years have seen a lot of baptisms, each with its own special memories, each with its own special joys. There was the baptism at Katolo which carried on through a drenching downpour. There was the baptism in the game park where a nervous Voice of Prophecy director loudly whispered to the pastor to baptize the candidates with their heads away from the nearby hippos. Here at Lukanga, many students have been through the waters of baptism and each has his own special story to tell.

My daughter, Heather, is eight and a half now. It won't be too long before she does some serious thinking about life. I hope it won't be too long before she decides to take that special step forward into baptism. When she does, you can be sure that somewhere in the front pews, there will be a proud mother and a proud father, and you can be sure that they will be brushing away the tears.

Yes, for some people, it's a wedding service that does it; for others, a funeral. For me, it's a baptism every time.

The Missionary Goes to Court

Masanga's trees were disappearing. There was no doubt about that. It was nothing very spectacular, and it wasn't happening very fast, but they were disappearing nonetheless. Every couple of days a new report would reach me in my office that a few more were gone.

"Nine, do you think we can catch the culprits?"

Nine's real name is Kendakenda. *Kenda* is Swahili for "nine," hence the nickname. Short of stature and slow to speak, Kendakenda was in charge of the school gardens. He was also in charge of the trees. Masanga planted them; Kendakenda and his crew weeded, thinned, and cut.

"Well," he said in his usual forthright manner, "it would have helped if you had done something about it back when the problem first started. There was probably only one person taking the trees then. Now, by the way they keep disappearing, I'd say there's quite a group."

He said it neither as an accusation or a condemnation, simply as a statement of fact. It was true, and I knew that I had only myself to blame for the burgeoning problem. Both Masanga and Kendakenda had come to me months before about the situation. But the school had acres of trees, and one can always expect a few to be taken, so I had let the matter slide. Now it looked as if I could have a major problem on my hands.

"OK, Nine," I said, "we'd better get this business stopped right now, once and for all. I want you to track down those thieves, even if you have to sleep in the woodlot. Keep your eyes on those trees and let me know if you see anything suspicious."

He looked at me thoughtfully, made a motion as if to reply, and then thought better of it. He headed for the door, paused, turned as if to speak, and thought better of it again. It was only as he stepped outside, one hand firmly gripping the door handle, that he found the courage to put his thoughts into words.

"When I find the thieves, I want you to bring them to court. I don't want to do all that work for nothing."

I was a bit surprised at his request, as we had never brought anyone to court before, but it made sense. If we could come down hard on these thieves, make of them an object lesson to others, a lot of our problems with petty thievery could be solved.

"All right," I acquiesced, "you catch them and I'll see to it that they go to court."

Within twenty-four hours, the thieves were caught. I heard a commotion outside the house and stepped out in time to see Kendakenda marching indignantly up the driveway with the shamefaced culprits following dutifully behind. They still had their machetes in their hands.

"Caught them in the act," he announced triumphantly. "They had two trees down and were working on a third when I found them."

As I looked at Kendakenda and at the thieves, I knew that I had gotten more than I had bargained for. This wasn't going to be easy. Kendakenda had done a superb job, all right, finding the thieves so quickly. But it hadn't been quite what I expected, and I didn't relish the idea of taking them to court. There were five of them, ranging in age from eight to sixty-five. All five were women.

"Nine," I asked unhappily, "what do you suggest?"
He didn't hesitate. "Let's go find the judge."
The trial began the next morning. It was a public one, held on the patch of ground in front of Mayele's store. Dozens, and perhaps hundreds, of spectators crowded around the table where the judges were seated. I had been expecting only one judge, the one we had seen the night before, but there were six of them at the table when the proceedings finally began.

A spokesman for the elderly six called the court to order. He looked first at the five women. "Do you agree to be judged by this court?" They all nodded their heads in agreement. They could hardly have refused, for the alternative was to go down to the chief's village and be tried by strangers, with soldiers standing guard. A trial in their own village, while far from pleasant, was much to be preferred.

"If you agree, throw down your money." Each of the women, in turn, threw five zaïres to the ground in front of her. One of the judges gave a signal, and an aide collected the bills. All of this was done with due respect for ceremonial procedure and was accompanied by much discussion among the lookers-on.

"Now, then, perhaps the principal of the school can explain to us why he has brought these women to court." The judge sounded as if he doubted the principal of the school had any explanation, and I had the feeling that most of the spectators doubted it too. I was suddenly aware of an unnatural silence that had descended over the crowd. Every eye was on me. This was the moment they had come to see. The missionary was about to take on five helpless women. As I looked at the expectant faces about me, a new realization began to dawn on my slow-working mind. I too was on trial. My future standing and influence with a lot of these people depended on the way I acquitted myself right now. I breathed a silent prayer for guidance, cleared my throat uneasily and prepared to speak. Just at that moment, Kendakenda leaned over and, like a defense lawyer advising his client, whispered urgently, "Don't say a thing!"

"What's up, Nine? Why shouldn't I talk?"

"That's not the way we do it here. Let me handle it."

Then he stood up and started explaining the situation. He spoke in Nande and, though it was impossible for me to follow it all, he was obviously making a favorable impression. When the judges questioned him, it was with deference. The crowd listened with respect. I breathed a sigh of relief and silently thanked him for taking control. He was handling a delicate situation much better than I ever could have. I knew that, thanks to him, my reputation would emerge intact.

The trial didn't follow the pattern I would have expected. To my surprise, any spectator was free to interrupt at any point with questions of his own if he wasn't satisfied with what the judges were asking. This happened on numerous occasions. The role of the judges seemed to be more one of coordination. They were there to keep things somewhat organized and to keep the whole procedure moving. This they did and, when at length the explanations were over and the last of the questions were asked, the judges turned to the women.

"What do you have to say for yourselves?"

They had nothing to say and just hung their heads in quiet shame. To all intents and purposes, it looked as if the trial was over at this point, but when the judges conferred among themselves, they decided they were not yet ready to reach a verdict. With much pomp and ceremony, the spokesman announced that there would be a recess of one hour to allow the judges to go to the woodlot and inspect the evidence personally.

Their decision met with general approval. It would have

been a letdown had the case been decided so quickly. It had become a major event, a bit of excitement in a slow week. Spirits were high and the arguments good-natured as the spectators tramped along behind the judges on the fifteen-minute walk up the hill.

When the scene of the crime had been duly examined and all the vast crowd had again found their places in front of Mayele's store, the proceedings resumed. This time, the judges announced at once that they were ready to pronounce sentence. There was no question of a verdict, for that was considered to be self-evident.

"Each women will pay the sum of one hundred zaïres to the school." The head judge looked directly at the women. "We hope you are ashamed of what you have done and will never do it again." He then looked at the spectators. "And let this be a lesson to each of you. If any of you are ever caught taking wood, you can be sure that you will be dealt with even more severely."

Finally, the judge turned to me. "You did a good thing in bringing your case before this court. Now we have just solved your problem for you, and it won't happen again. That we know. But you must do one last thing. There was dew on the grass when we walked up to inspect the trees. We had to walk through it. Pay us costs of fifteen zaïres for the purchase of shoe polish. Court is dismissed."

He sat down with a flourish, and I couldn't help but look at the six pairs of feet protruding from beneath the table. One judge was wearing thongs. The other five pairs of feet were bare.

Court costs were duly paid, and the women borrowed from friends and family and took care of the fines. The spectators moved off in small groups and wandered away. Justice had been meted out, and everyone was satisfied. But whether the shoe polish was ever applied, well, that I can only guess.

The Walls Came Tumbling Down

I could see by the expression on Kihungu's face that he was not convinced. "You say you want us to make a room under the ground? With another room on top? Maybe if we waited until Carscallen came back—"

That was just the point. I didn't want to wait until Carscallen came back. He was certain to have his own ideas as to how the work should be done, and I had a strong feeling he would veto the entire project.

We were building a second storage room for the school cafeteria. The original plan was to build it beside the existing one, but it had seemed to me, after a few quick calculations, that it would be cheaper to build it directly under the existing one. The way I saw it, this would save both roofing materials and ground space. Carey Carscallen would normally have been consulted about a change of this nature, but he was home on furlough and wouldn't be back until the school year had started. Cellars are virtually unknown in these parts, and I decided it would be an ideal opportunity to introduce them. Kihungu wasn't so sure.

For years, Kihungu has been head mason at Lukanga. He is a little giant of a man—short, stocky, barrel-chested. His personality is that of so many of the Nande—easy-going, good-natured, relaxed. He is a skilled workman and is respected by his men. Under his guidance, the masonry work was done for the technical school, for the two churches, for almost all of the houses, and for the new girls' dorm. But none of those buildings involved a cellar, and Kihungu scratched his head vigorously as he puzzled over the problem.

"Where is the door going to be? If this room is under the ground, isn't it going to be a bit hard to get in?"

I sighed. Fulton had his scoffers, and it appeared I would have mine. "We'll make an outside entrance with stairs going down."

He could still foresee problems. "And what about the rain? How do we stop it from coming in?"

"We'll build a covering over the stairway."

"And what will we do for light?"

My patience was beginning to wear thin. It was not that I was upset with Kihungu as such, but I was growing ever more exasperated with the projected hole in the ground. It had seemed so easy when I first thought of it, and I had somehow assumed the details would take care of themselves. But they weren't, and Kihungu wanted answers.

As I looked at him standing there, I could tell he still wasn't satisfied. He was clutching his wool knit cap between his hands and grinning, but the furrows in his forehead revealed his perplexity.

"I guess you'll explain that part when we get to it," he said at length. "Besides, maybe Carscallen will be back by then."

There it was again. That same lack of confidence. Still, he had offered me a face-saving way out of the present discussion, and I accepted it gratefully. "Right. We'll work out that part when we get to it. First, let's get the hole dug."

Wasukundi soon tracked down a man to dig the hole, and within days, all was ready for the masons. They went to work with a will and soon finished three of the walls. These were set in a foot or so from the walls in the storage room above to keep from undermining those. The fourth wall was more of a problem. This was where the door was to go. A ramp would have to be dug for the outside stairway, and it would have to be dug right under the foundations above. I planned it so the cellar door would be directly under the door above and we dug the ramp. The masons built the wall, and the carpenters built the double doorframe. So far, so good, but now the problems began in earnest. What kind of a structure could we build to give access to the upper room, access to the outside stairway and no access to the rain?

I was still debating the question when Carey came back from furlough. Time had run out. He wanted a tour around to see what had been happening, and there was nowhere I could hide that hole. He reacted with characteristic calm.

"What's the hole for, Bob? You hoping to catch rain water in there?"

I laughed uneasily and felt my face turn red. "Well, no, not really. It's a root cellar. I thought it would be just the thing for storing palm oil and the like. But we've got a slight problem. We haven't figured out just how to build the outside stairway. I was hoping to have it done before you got back, but we didn't quite make it."

That last statement was hardly necessary. It was abundantly clear that we hadn't quite made it, and Carey paused to study the situation. He walked around the hole, hesitated, and then went down the ramp to study it from within. I followed along behind, embarrassed and painfully aware of how it must look to him—a gaping hole where once a storage room had been. After what seemed forever, he announced his decision.

"There's not much we can do about the hole itself. I'm not sure I'd have put an underground room here. But since it's already done we'd better make a few little changes. That outside ramp will never work. I think we should build an additional storage room at ground level beside the present one. Then we can build a ramp inside there. That way we'll have no problem with rain, and the whole thing will look a lot better."

I am sure Kihungu was tempted to say, "I told you so," when I informed him of the change in plans the next morning, but if so, he kept it to himself. He simply raised his eyebrows affirmatively, and his only comment was the long, drawn-out "Ayyyy!" which indicates agreement among the Nande.

It took only a day or so for the masons to take out the door frame and brick up the wall. They threw dirt back where the outside stairway was to have gone and soon removed all traces of their previous work. I think they were just as relieved as I was to be done with the embarrassing ramp, but if they thought they had seen the last of it, they were soon to be proven wrong. The ramp was to have the last word yet.

A week later, the rain began. It fell in torrents for days. Mud spattered our clothes as we walked, and it oozed around our feet. It pulled at shoes and boots with its slimy grip. It completely covered the construction site. Work was impossible. The masons huddled in makeshift shelters around smoky fires when it rained. They slipped in the mud when it stopped.

This went on for a week until, finally, the weather cleared. The sun came out and it looked as if things might dry up. Kihungu and his crew went back to work with fresh energy. I saw them cheerfully laying bricks for the new room as I walked by on the way to class. Kihungu was wearing his wool knit cap, as usual, and keeping up a steady chatter.

When I came back from my classes several hours later, I saw all the masons standing around in a forlorn-looking group. I started over to see what had happened but stopped short in amazement. The ramp was back and the wall was gone. Evidently, as the rains had continued to fall, the dirt fill over the ramp had turned to mud. Gradually, the pressure built until at last the whole thing slid down into our newly-built cellar.

Nobody was hurt when the wall caved in, although my pride suffered yet another blow. Kihungu clutched his cap ever more tightly as he told me what had happened. This time, the look in his eye was unmistakable, he didn't need to say a word. Every brick in that jumbled heap at the bottom of the hole said it for him: "I told you so."

The root cellar is in regular use now. It will be an unusually observant visitor who notices the double wall on the side where the outside ramp once was. The inner ramp works well. The masons were able to salvage a cement header from the cave-in. It had gone above the upper door and it somehow held together when the wall came tumbling down. It has since been installed over the door into the new room. I helped the masons hoist it into place myself.

From time to time I still get the urge to rush things through without asking the experts and taking care of the details first. I suppose it's a weakness I'll have all my life, but these days I have an antedote. All I have to do is look over at the cafeteria storage room. The old cement header is still in its place and as long as it is, it'll always remind me of Kihungu and an experience I don't care to go through again.

Mrs. Nzabamwita's Special Sabbath Dinner

Under different circumstances, the table spread before me would have had my mouth watering, for Mrs. Nzabamwita had prepared a meal fit for a king. There was a dazzlingly white rice entree with a sauce of tomatoes, leeks, and garlic. There were great heaps of boiled potatoes, garnished lightly with unknown herbs. There was a peanut sauce, a tossed salad, and ground cassava leaves. There was fresh-baked bread and corn on the cob. All in all, it was a meal such as one rarely finds in these parts.

I had been eating on my own for some time—a new experience for me after seven years of marriage and Diane's good cooking. Diane had gone back to Canada to have the latest addition to the family, and I had to rough it for four months. Pickings were slim on my own table. I often woke up at night to find I had been dreaming about food. By all rights, I should have been able to do justice to the feast spread before me, but there was just one problem. I had already eaten.

To this day I'm not sure how I forgot about the invitation. Mrs. Nzabamwita had asked me well in advance, and I had been looking forward to the meal for the entire week. She had a reputation for cooking which was known across campus and, if the quality of her cooking was legendary, it was for sheer quantity that she was most renowned. She

MRS. NZABAMWITA'S SPECIAL SABBATH DINNER   85

was one of those who believe that if a little is good, then a lot is better. Her dinner table—on Sabbaths at least— fairly groaned under the burden it bore.

She was an interesting person, Mrs. Nzabamwita, and just a little hard to get to know. Her husband was pastor of the church and she was the head deaconess. She always sat rigidly in her pew throughout the service, except when the collection plate was passed, for, in what was considered to be quite an innovation for a woman, she helped collect the offerings. As her stern gaze swept down the rows, offerings were hastily deposited and the collection plate passed along. There was no dawdling, and her half of the church was invariably done well before the other. At communion services, she folded the covering cloth with the same grim precision she brought to almost everything she did. It was somewhat surprising, then, to find that behind the forbidding facade was a warm and caring person.

It was through her cooking that Mrs. Nzabamwita expressed herself most easily and most eloquently, as many a hungry and homesick student soon learned. She was a master in the kitchen and there, in more relaxed surroundings, her personality underwent a complete transformation. Sternness dissolved into softness, and grimness gave way to giggling. She kept her own large gardens around the house, and it was her own produce that appeared on her table. Perhaps it was this that allowed her to prepare so much, for her husband's salary was not large. But her meals were, and they brought to her Sabbath noons the delight which was so conspicuously absent in the mornings.

Walking back from church on the Sabbath of my invitation, I fell into an animated discussion with Dick Roos. Dick was our mission director at the time, having preceded Dave Saguan at the post. He was a veritable fountain of ideas. By the time we reached his home, I was totally immersed in the conversation. Dinner had been prepared before church and before I fully realized what was happening, we were sitting at the table eating, as the discussion continued.

Dick's wife, Bonnie, was a strong believer in simple cooking. Her meals were often built around grain products such as bread, which she made from wheat she ground herself. She was a skilled and experienced cook and her meals were both nutritious and tasty. They did, nonetheless, sit very heavily in the stomach. By the time I had finished eating, I had lost interest in conversation and wanted only a comfortable place in which to recline. Not that I would be sleeping it off. My sleep mechanism, or whatever it is that controls such things, can never be tricked by a full stomach and only goes into effect after dark. No, it would be an afternoon of leisurely reading, followed by picture-roll evangelism with the students.

As I walked along the road, heading to the office for some reading material, I passed Pastor Nzabamwita's house. My reflexes had been dulled by the heavy meal; when I saw the pastor waving to me from the doorway, there was a moment's delay before I realized what I had done.

"Come on in. You're just in time. The wife has a bit of food ready, and she's just put it on the table."

At those portentous words, "a bit of food," the full realization of what was in store came flooding over me. I had already eaten more than enough to see me through the day and well into the next one, but there was no backing out now. I could well imagine the feast which the lady of the house must have prepared and which the man of the house described so casually as "a bit of food."

I stepped into the house and as I passed through the kitchen, a blast of heat struck me with withering force. The top of the wood stove was covered with various pots and casseroles, bubbling and whistling merrily, lids jumping and dancing to the soft hiss of escaping steam. Everywhere I looked there was food in preparation—rice and potatoes, breads and greens. Mrs. Nzabamwita had pulled out all the stops to make this a meal to remember. And it was. I don't suppose I shall ever forget that meal as long as I live.

I have offered prayers many times in my life and under many different circumstances, but seldom were any more fervent and more heartfelt than my prayer that day in silent accompaniment to the pastor's. He prayed for blessings on the food and on those who had prepared it. I prayed for something else—an appetite. Gluttony may be one of the seven deadly sins, but it was a vice I longed for as I raised my fork and began to eat.

The first course went better than I could have hoped. I took a lot of salad and, accompanied by a delicious peanut sauce, the rice slid down with amazing ease. There was no question about it. All of that good woman's heart and soul and energy had gone into the preparation of this food, and she had turned out a work of art.

I reviewed my options. To refuse was to offend. I wouldn't have offended Mrs. Nzabamwita for anything in the world, so that was out. I would have slipped a little off my plate, onto my lap, onto the floor, under my shirt—anywhere—but there was never any chance. She hovered over me constantly, like an attentive waiter in a swanky restaurant, suggesting dishes and watching for my reactions. There was no way out.

I ate slowly and dawdled as much as possible, but whenever I managed to down the tiny portion I had put on my plate, she delightedly filled it up again. There was no refusing her; it was pointless to try. I plunged bravely on until the room and everyone in it faded gradually into a hazy blur. I could feel the temperature rising. I began to perspire freely, and my vague attempts at conversation made less and less sense, even to me.

I remember very little about the rest of the meal. The memory has dimmed and all that remains in my mind is the dulled image of mountains of food, an indistinct mix of odors and flavors, and a feeling of bloat. I do know that somehow I managed to finish without offending my hostess, for when I finally staggered drunkenly out her door, aiming myself in the general direction of home, she was standing in the doorway, beaming and watching my departure with an unmistakable look of pride.

The teachers and the students spent the afternoon holding evangelistic meetings in the neighboring villages. I spent it, in spite of myself, sound asleep in bed. I woke up just in time to see the little preaching groups coming back. I watched them for a few minutes and then turned back to bed. As I again drifted off to sleep, it was without any feelings of guilt. I knew that I too had done my missionary work for the afternoon.

Home at Last! But Africa Has Our Hearts!

It was good to be home. Three years in the mission field were at an end, three more were yet to begin. It was time to step back and get things into perspective. They had been good years, by far the most exciting of our lives, and they had slipped by far too quickly. All, that is, except for the last few months.

Diane and the children had gone on ahead of me in January. I didn't make it to Canada until June. How we survived, I don't know. It wasn't easy. They say home is where you hang your hat, but they're wrong. Home is where your family is. Lukanga had been home, but once they left, well, I couldn't wait to get to Canada again.

I had a little surprise for Diane when I arrived—a beard. She had a little surprise for me—a son. These things were momentarily overlooked, of course, during the preliminary greetings. It was several minutes before we got around to talking. I broke the silence first.

"What's his name, Diane?"

She thought I was kidding. "You know his name. We agreed on it before we left."

"Yes, but we were expecting a girl, remember? I hope you haven't called him Christie."

She laughed. "Mr. Prouty, meet your son, Edward Roy."

Just then, as if on cue, Edward Roy sleepily opened his eyes and yawned. I took him happily in my arms, held him to my cheek, and rocked him slowly back and forth. We were in the middle of the airport, people were swarming all around, and we had a long drive ahead of us, but I wasn't going to be rushed. This moment had been five months coming, and it was going to be savored.

Furlough was hectic, but exciting. It might be an exaggeration to say we went everywhere and did everything, but it is certain we saw a lot of new places and met a lot of new friends. And yet, for all that, one of the most exciting moments of the entire summer happened right at home in College Park Church in Oshawa. A lot of my earliest and fondest memories come from the Sabbath School rooms and pews in that church. I was there for the very first service ever held in the church. My brother and I remember it well. We were in the choir.

Don was in grade four at the time; I was a year behind. The whole elementary school had been asked to sing, and at the final rehearsal, our teacher called Don and me aside and told us we had a special role to play. To be singled out from all that vast assemblage was quite an honor, and we felt it keenly. We listened to her instructions with special care. We were to be the "mouthers." We were not to sing like all the others. We were to mouth the words and make it look like we were singing.

Don and I had a good time that Sabbath. We sang with our hearts, but we didn't make a sound. After the service, we heard a number of people telling our teacher that the choir had sounded great. We looked at one another and smiled with quiet pride. We knew we had done our part.

There are other days at College Park that stand out in my mind, days I'll never forget. I remember the time Frank Buchanan, in the middle of the Sabbath School secretary's report, leaned over and lost his glasses in a crack behind the pulpit. Mr. Buchanan, an intensely interesting man at any time, never held our interest as he did that day. He couldn't read a thing without those glasses, and for five minutes the whole Sabbath School came to a halt while the deacons tried to retrieve them. They succeeded at last, but not before another day had been forever enshrined in local history.

Our big day during furlough happened during Sabbath School too. Again the proceedings were interrupted; again I was there to enjoy it all. This time, I was the one in the pulpit. I had been giving the mission story.

I spoke that morning about the church they used to call the Ngumbe church. It's about a three-hour walk from Lukanga, with a membership composed largely of elderly women. There are several well-built churches in the area, and the women at Ngumbe decided that their church should be upgraded. They got together and started carrying rocks. Every Sunday, week after week, month after month, they carried rocks on their heads up to the site where the church was to be built. They carried enough rocks to build not only the foundation of the church but also all four of the walls. A member of our church at Lukanga paid for the masons.

One day, as I visited the church, I said to one of the older women, "You certainly are lucky to have so many rocks nearby."

"Yes," she agreed, "we were lucky."

"But just where do you get them from," I continued, somewhat puzzled because I could see no quarry.

She shrugged and pointed. "Down there."

I looked. "Down there!" I gasped. Those old women had gotten their rocks from a riverbed, one and a quarter stair-steep miles away. That they could even negotiate such a path was astonishing. How had they carried so many rocks! They had brought literally thousands of them. The church walls were two feet thick; there was room inside for hundreds of people. To my way of thinking, the pyramids themselves had little to teach these women. But the pyramids had been finished; the church had not. The rocks had been hauled, the walls had been built, and there, sadly, the project had stopped. The poor women had no way of putting on a roof. Roofs cost money; they had none. They had done what they could, and now they could do no more. They had been waiting for three years.

I never finished my story that morning. One of the church members suddenly stood up. I recognized Mrs. Sowers, the former college president's wife.

"Bob," she said, "what can we do to help those dear old ladies?"

Let no one ever say that a big church has to be a cold church. I learned differently that day. I had intended no direct appeal for money for this church, the one they used to call the Ngumbe church. But Mrs. Sowers and her friends had something more specific in mind. Before I left church that morning, she told me that they had made up their minds. They were going to raise the roof.

Raise the roof they did. By the end of our furlough, thousands of dollars had been raised, all of it unsolicited. Not only did the women at Ngumbe get a roof on their church, but three other churches got one as well.

There is very little that has touched my heart more than the way those people gave that summer. One woman sold her washing machine to raise funds. Mr. West, the school janitor, organized the students to sell candy bars. The folks in the retirement home nearby, raised so much that the church was named after the home. It used to be called the Ngumbe church. Now it's the Pioneer Homes Church. Old folks in Canada helping old folks in Africa. It's a small world, after all.

It wasn't just the College Park Church which helped, of

HOME AT LAST! BUT AFRICA HAS OUR HEARTS! 93

course. The church members from nearby Bowmanville sent package after package of much-needed clothing, and the people in Diane's hometown of Monroe, Michigan, helped in countless little ways. And then, later that summer, the whole thing happened again. Much to our surprise, lightning struck for the second time, though admittedly not in the same place.

We were attending the Quebec camp meeting, and Mrs. Violet Hall, a well-known Canadian educator, who had charge of the juniors, asked me to tell a story in that division. I could hardly refuse, since she has known me longer than I have known myself, but I didn't know what I was in for. Half of those juniors spoke English; the other half spoke French. There was no one there to translate, so, for the first time in my life, I did it myself. One sentence in French, one sentence in English. It was a unique experience. But what happened next was not. It had already happened in Oshawa.

Mrs. Hall had been listening quietly, but she suddenly sprang to her feet. "Children," she said, "I think this is wonderful. Now what are we going to do about it? Wouldn't you like to help?" They assured her they would.

"All right, then, you go back to your tents or your cars or wherever it is that your parents are, and you tell them that Granny Hall says you can't come back until they've given something to help their friends in Africa." With that, the juniors gave an enthusiastic whoop, rushed for the door, and were gone.

Moments earlier I had been addressing a full room. Now it was empty. Chairs were turned this way and that, just as they had been left in the headlong rush for the door. No one remained, except for Mrs. Hall and me. She was just standing there, looking out the door, excited and pleased with herself.

"Mrs. Hall," I protested, "you can't do this."

"Don't be silly," she said. "Of course I can."

"But what about the conference president? He said he would be stopping by. What will he say when he finds out what you're doing?"

She looked upset. "I forgot the conference president. I should have asked him first."

Soon the children began wandering back in, offerings in hand. Then the conference president arrived. I could tell he was wondering what was going on. I looked at Mrs. Hall to see how she would handle it. She didn't hesitate for a second.

"Now, Pastor Sabot," she said, "we're not letting anyone into this room without an offering for Africa. I was just telling Bob that I should have asked you first, but you weren't here so I'm asking you now. How much would you like to give?"

It was late that night before we finally said the last goodbyes and headed back for home. Among the donations we carefully tucked away before driving off was a generous one from Pastor Sabot. He was happy to give, he said, and besides, Mrs. Hall was a very persuasive woman.

He could have added "warm-hearted" too. Typical of the people we met all during furlough. We had felt so far away from them all for so long. It had been fun in the mission field, and it would be good to be back, but for now we were enjoying a very special feeling. We had found our church family again. It was good to be home.